PICTURE BOOK OF CUTE DOGS

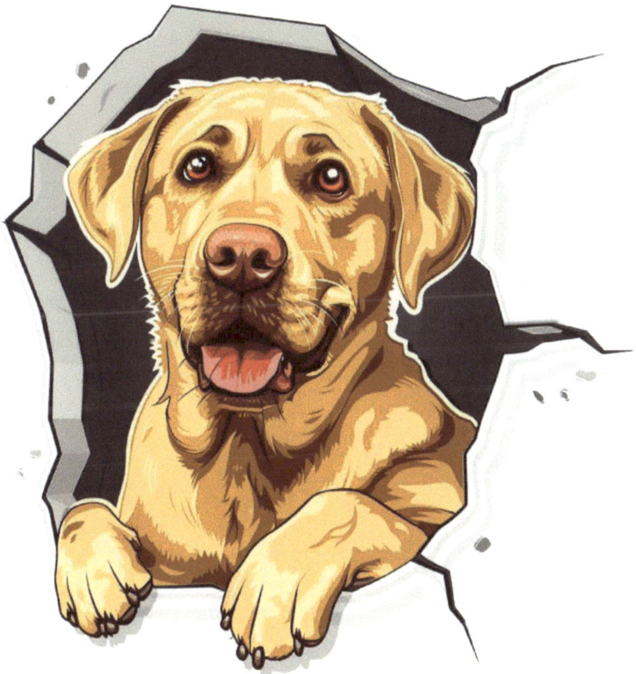

...By...

Ella Caldwell

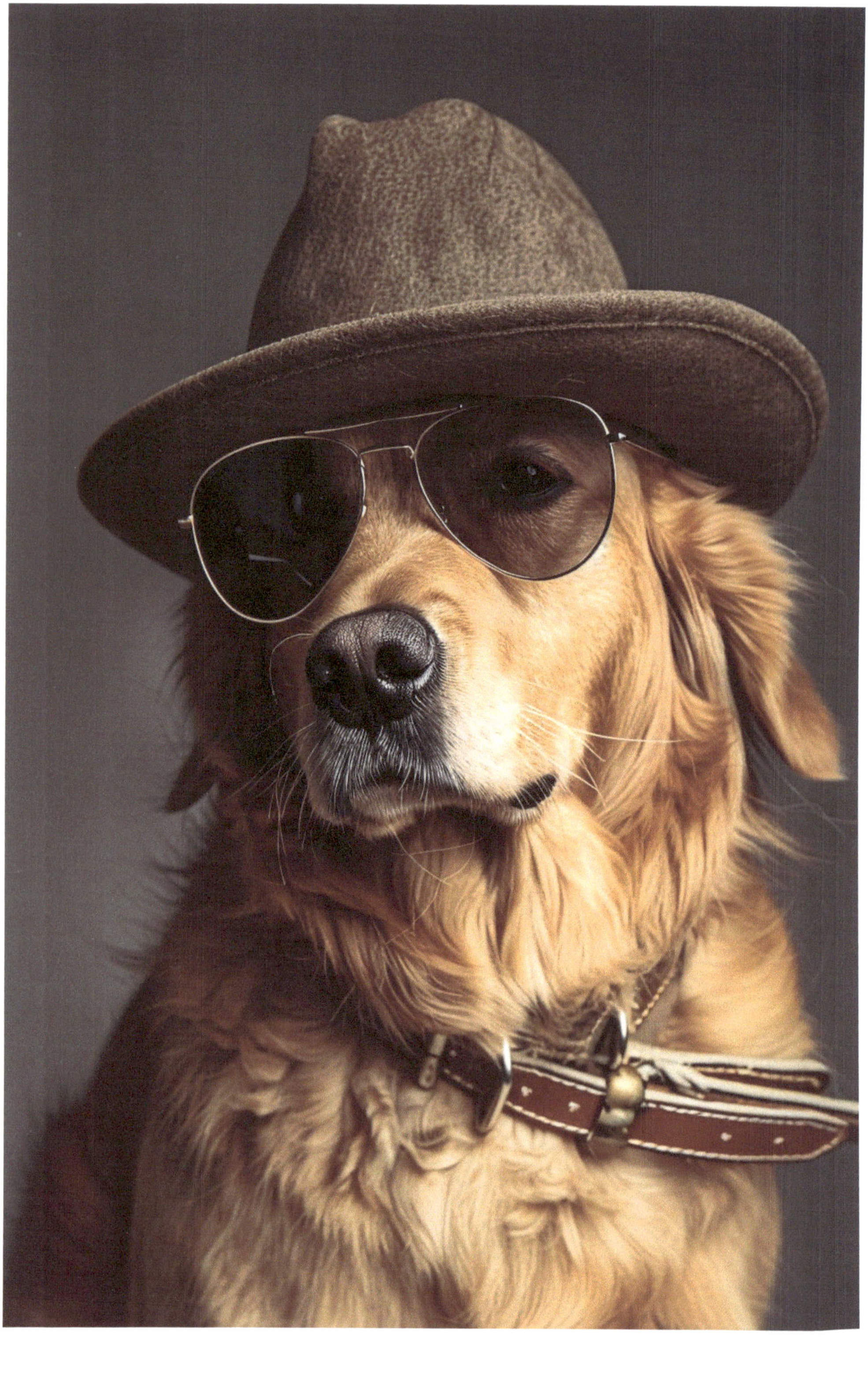

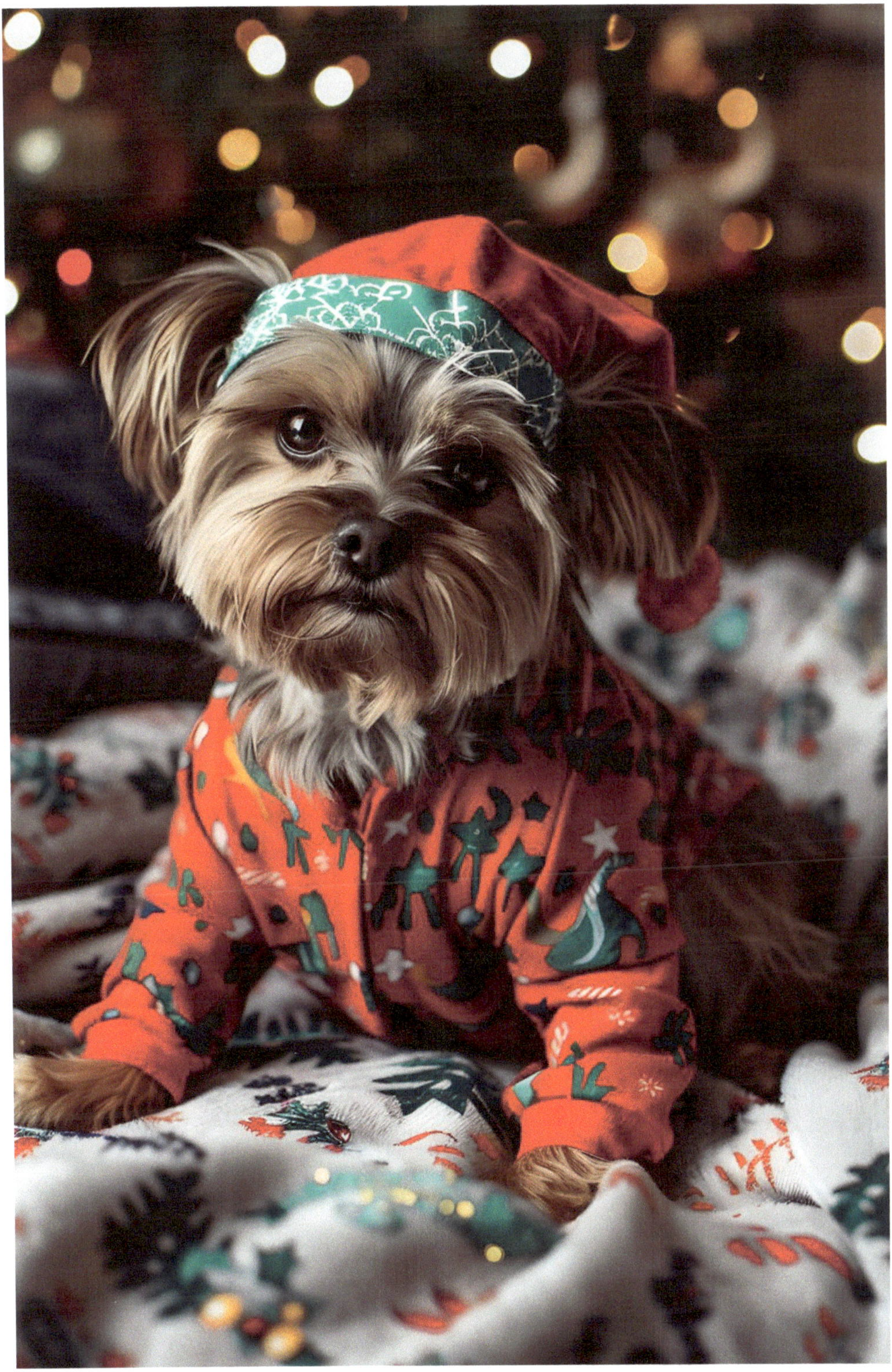

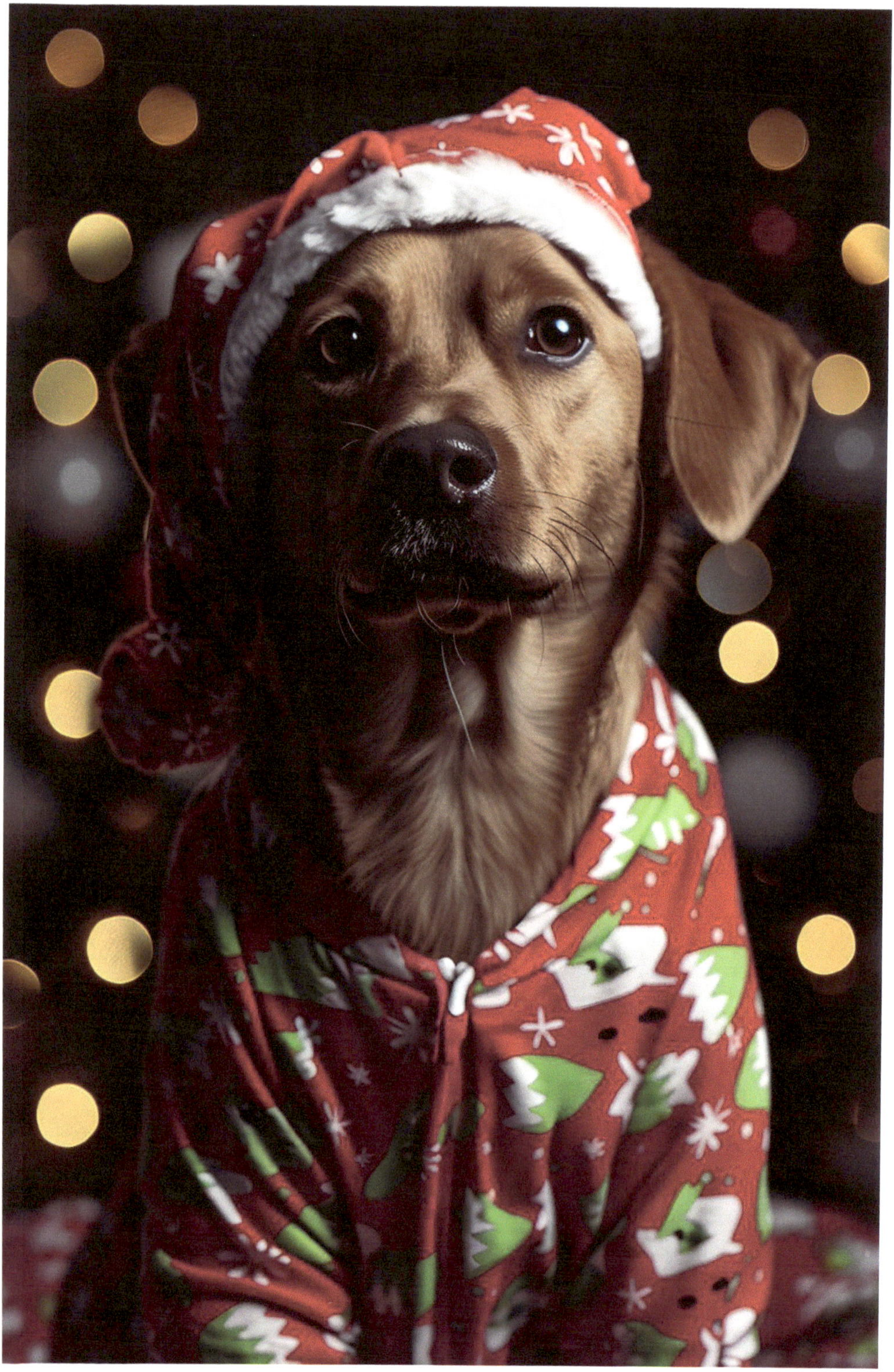

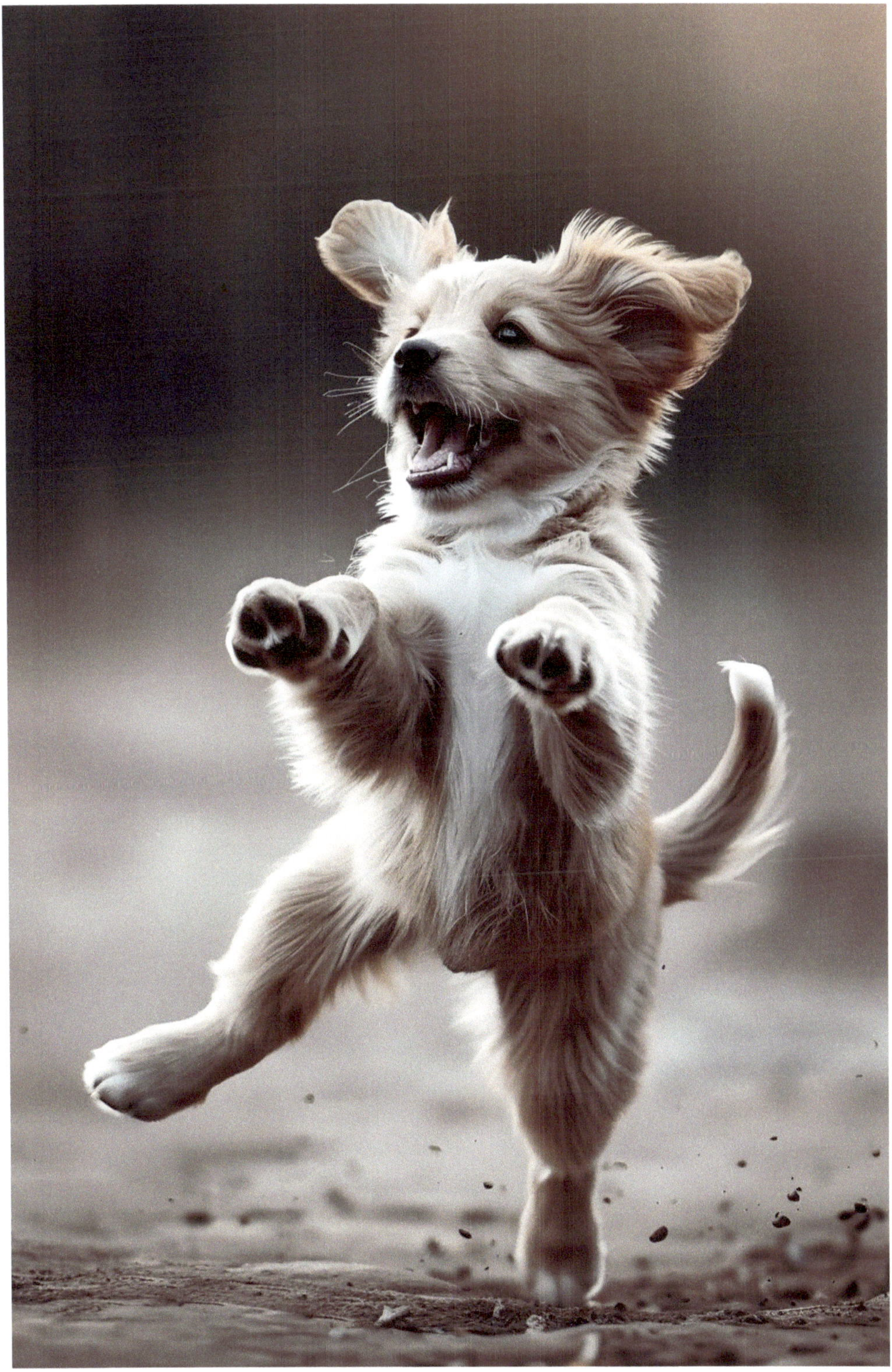

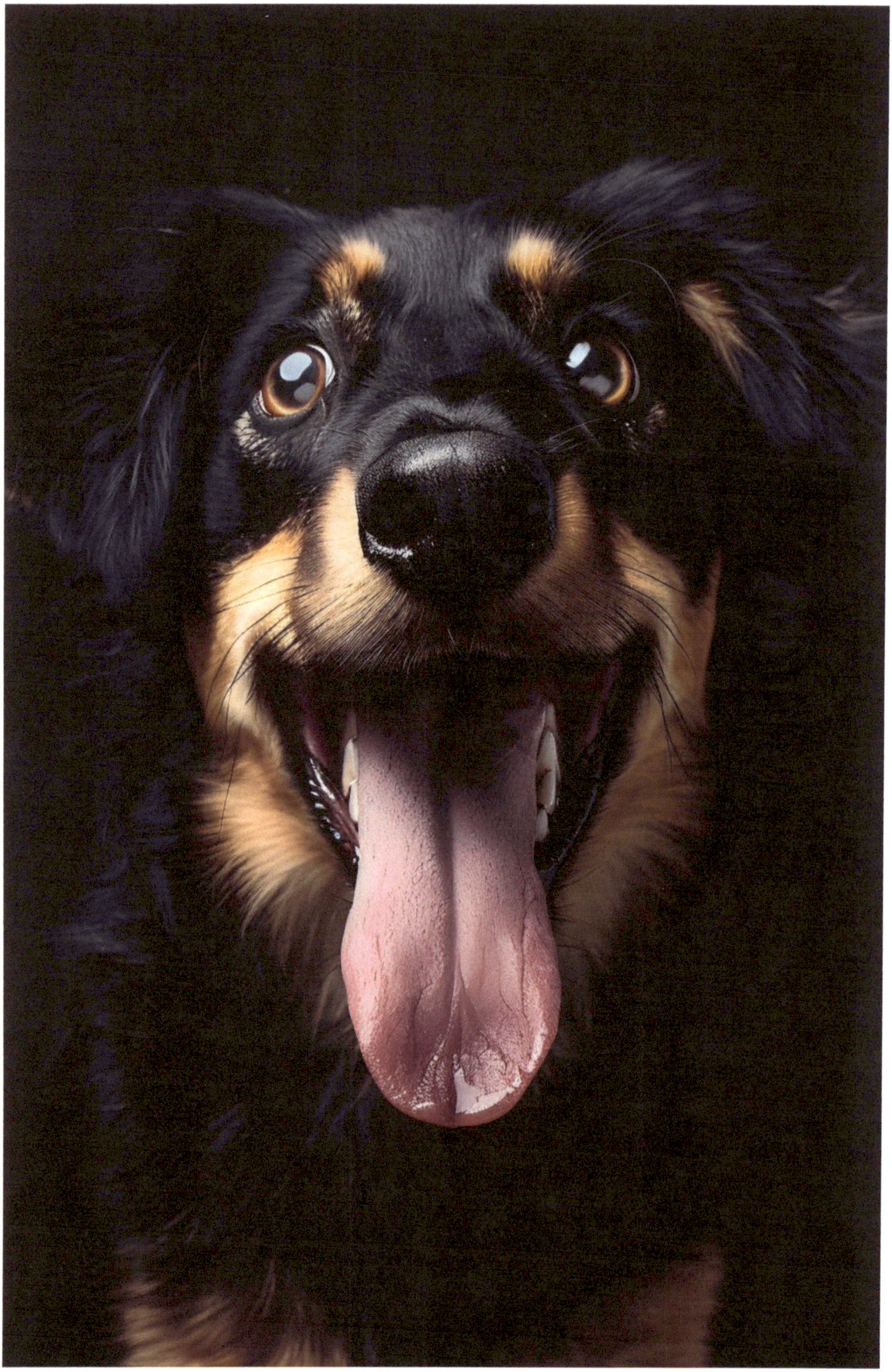

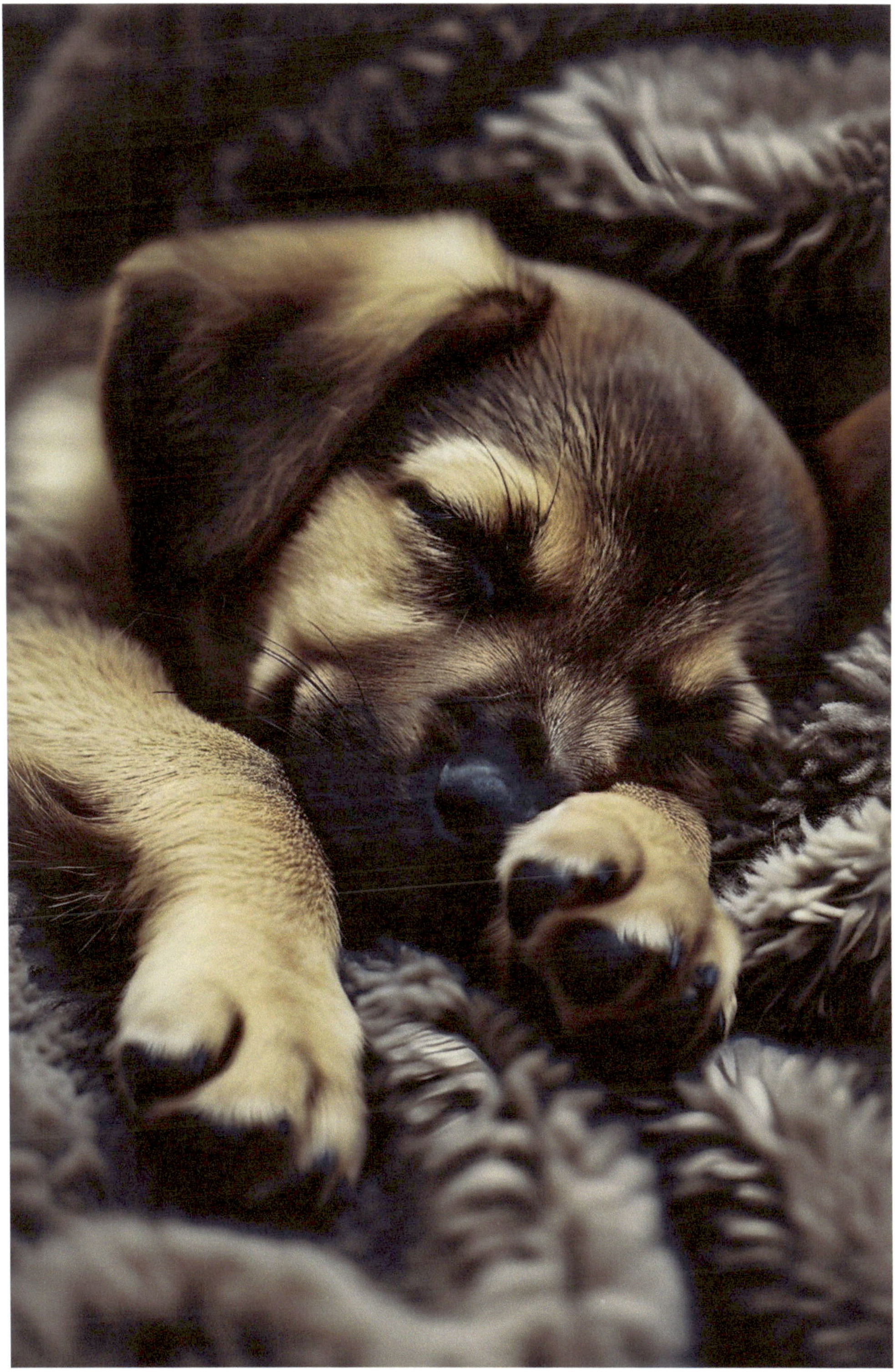

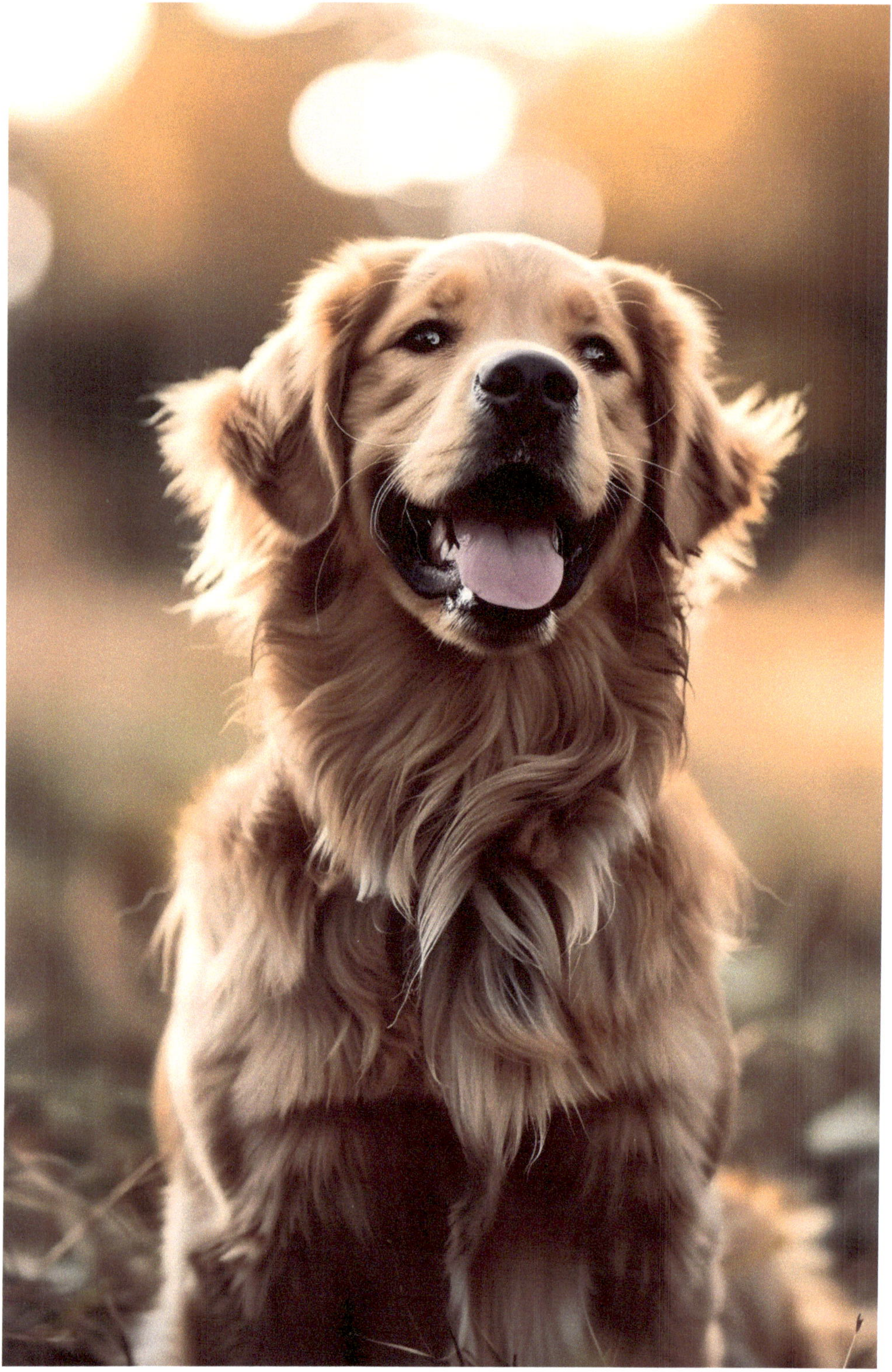

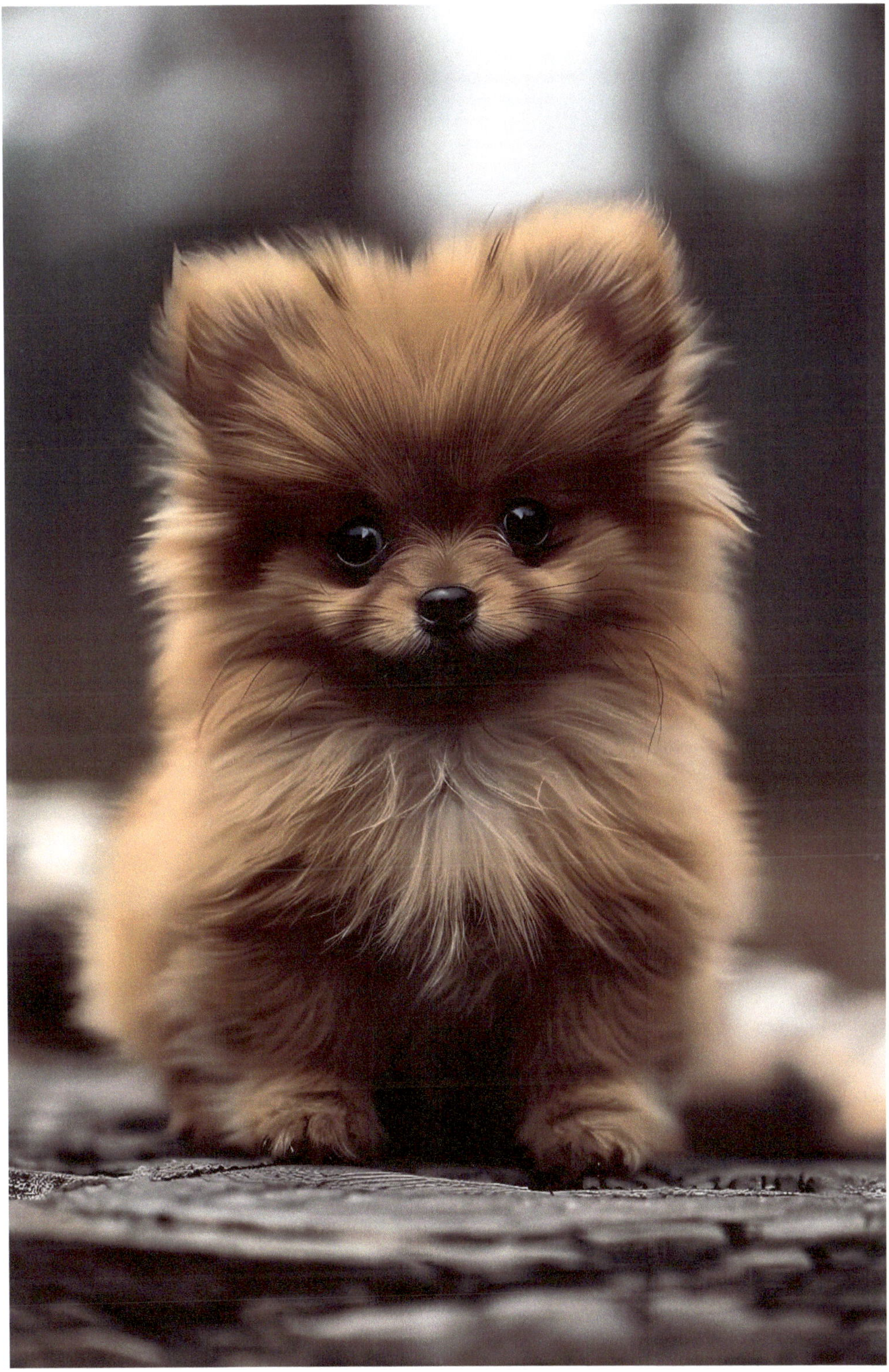

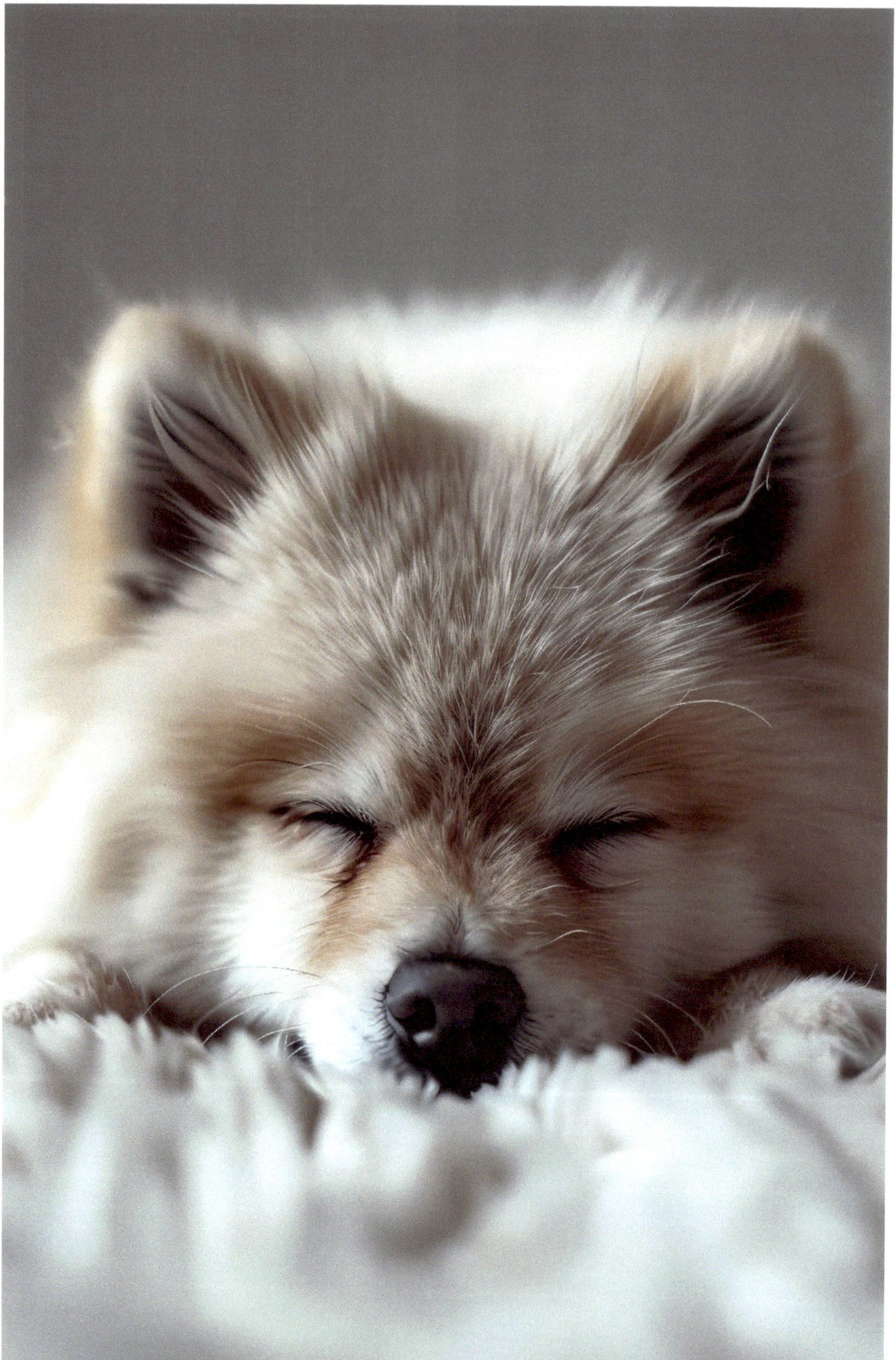

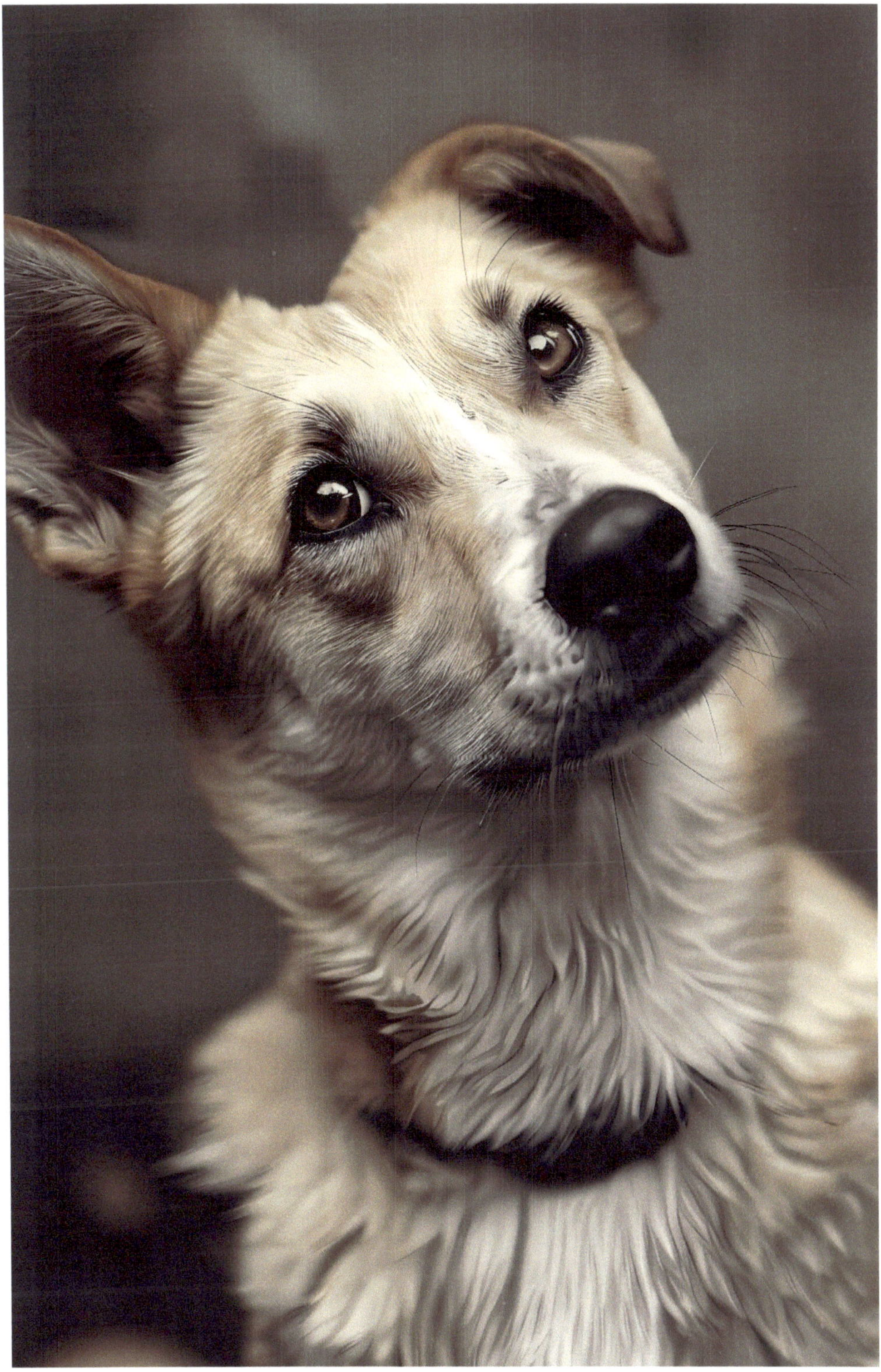

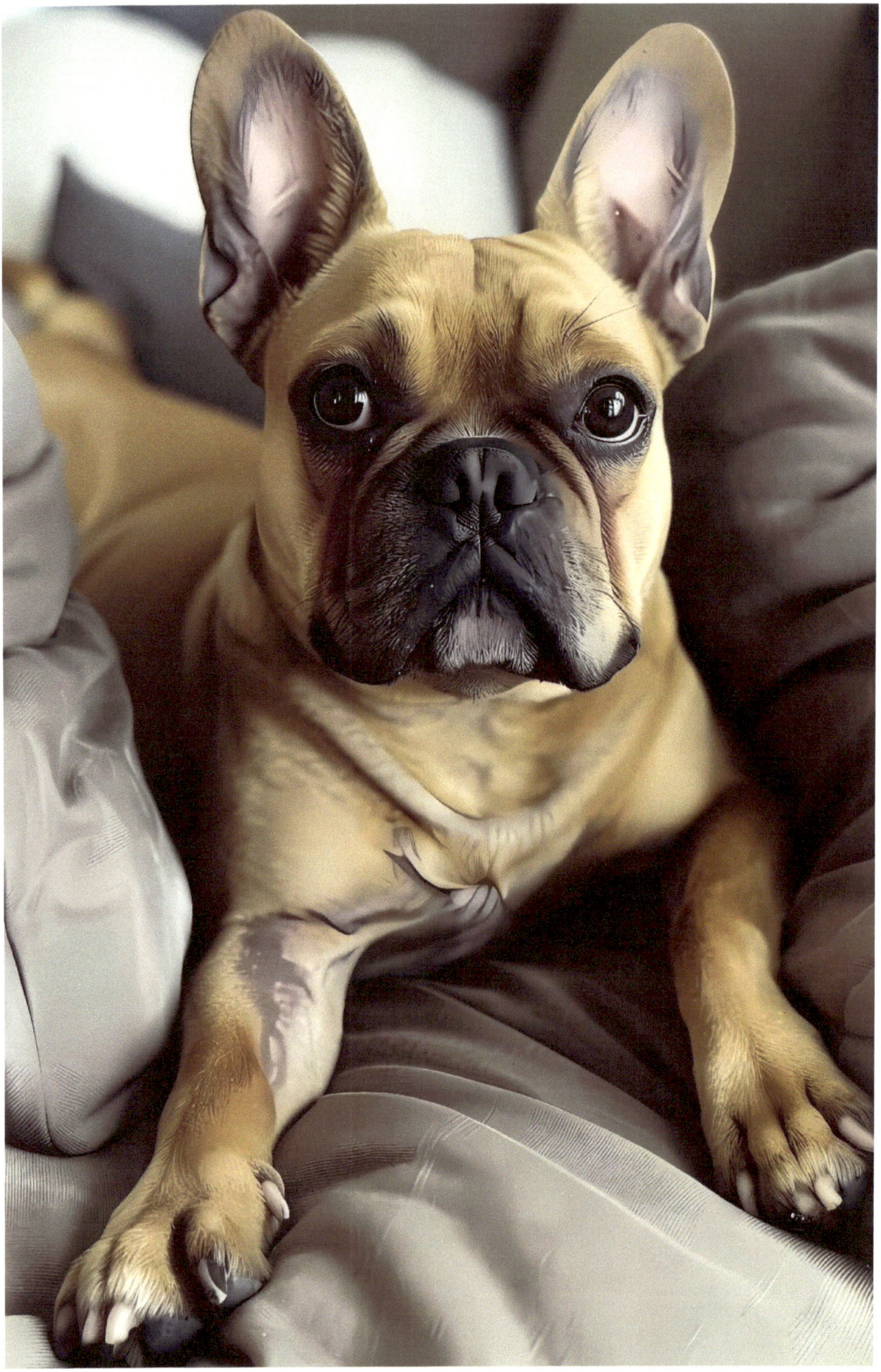

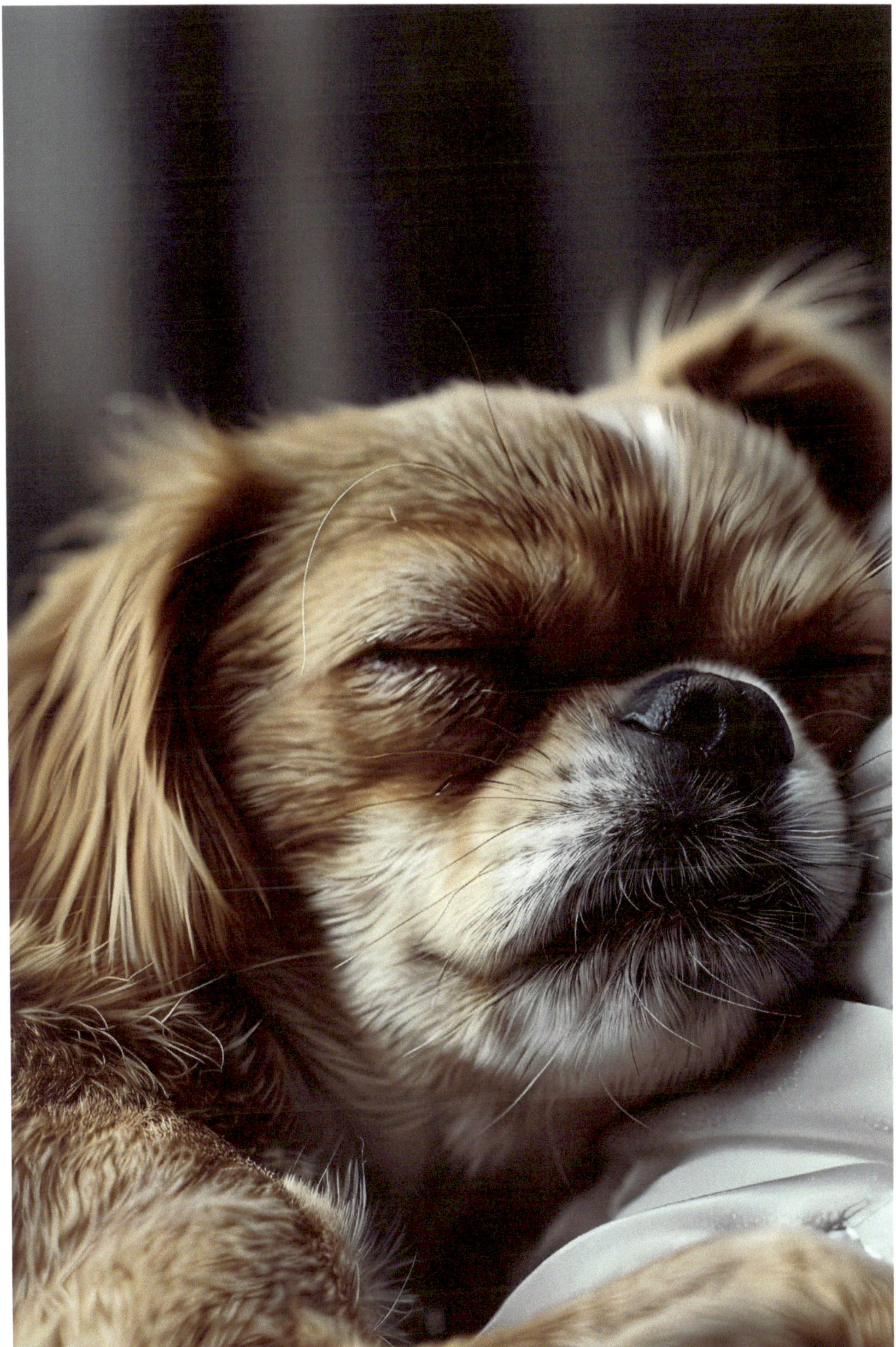

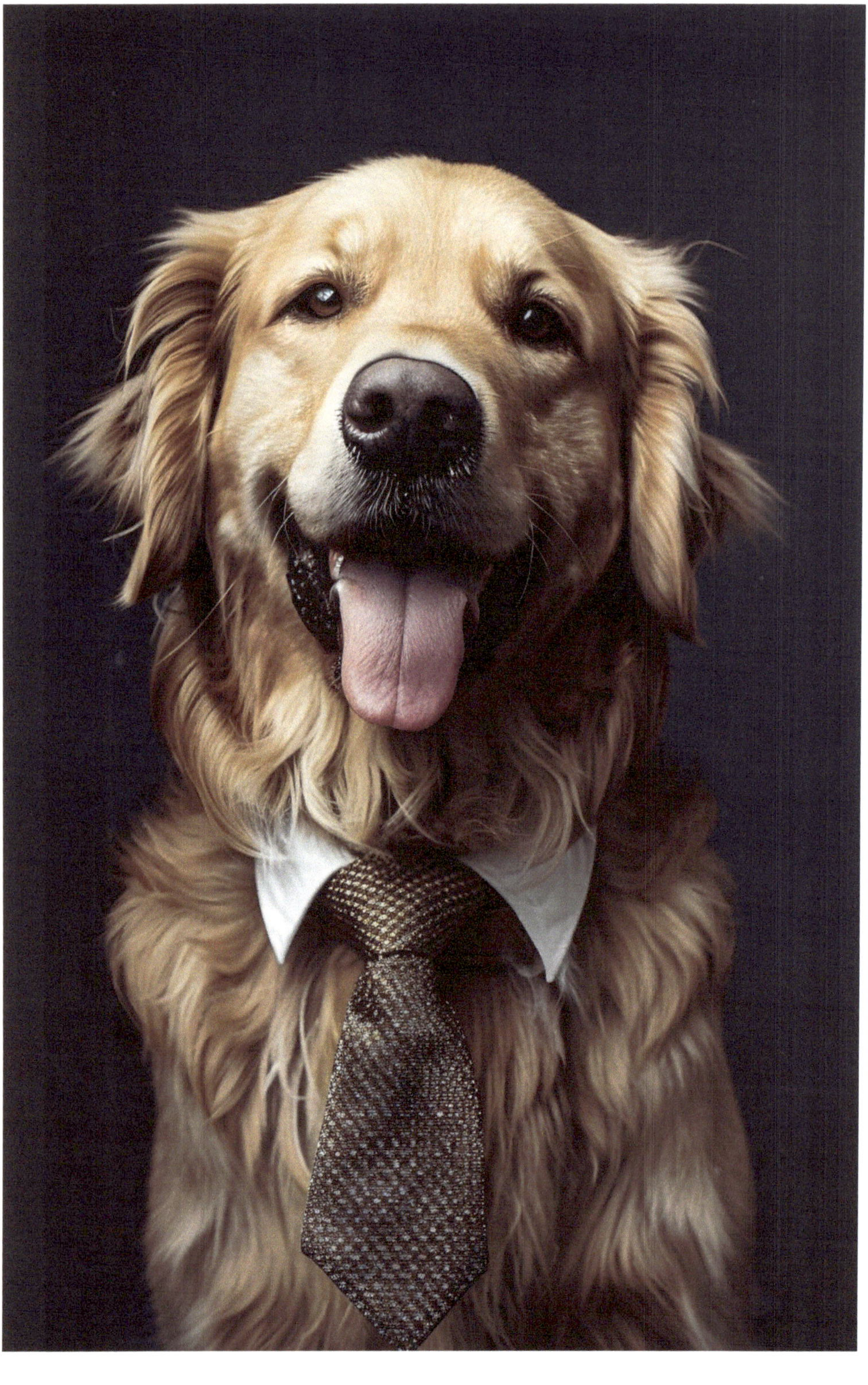

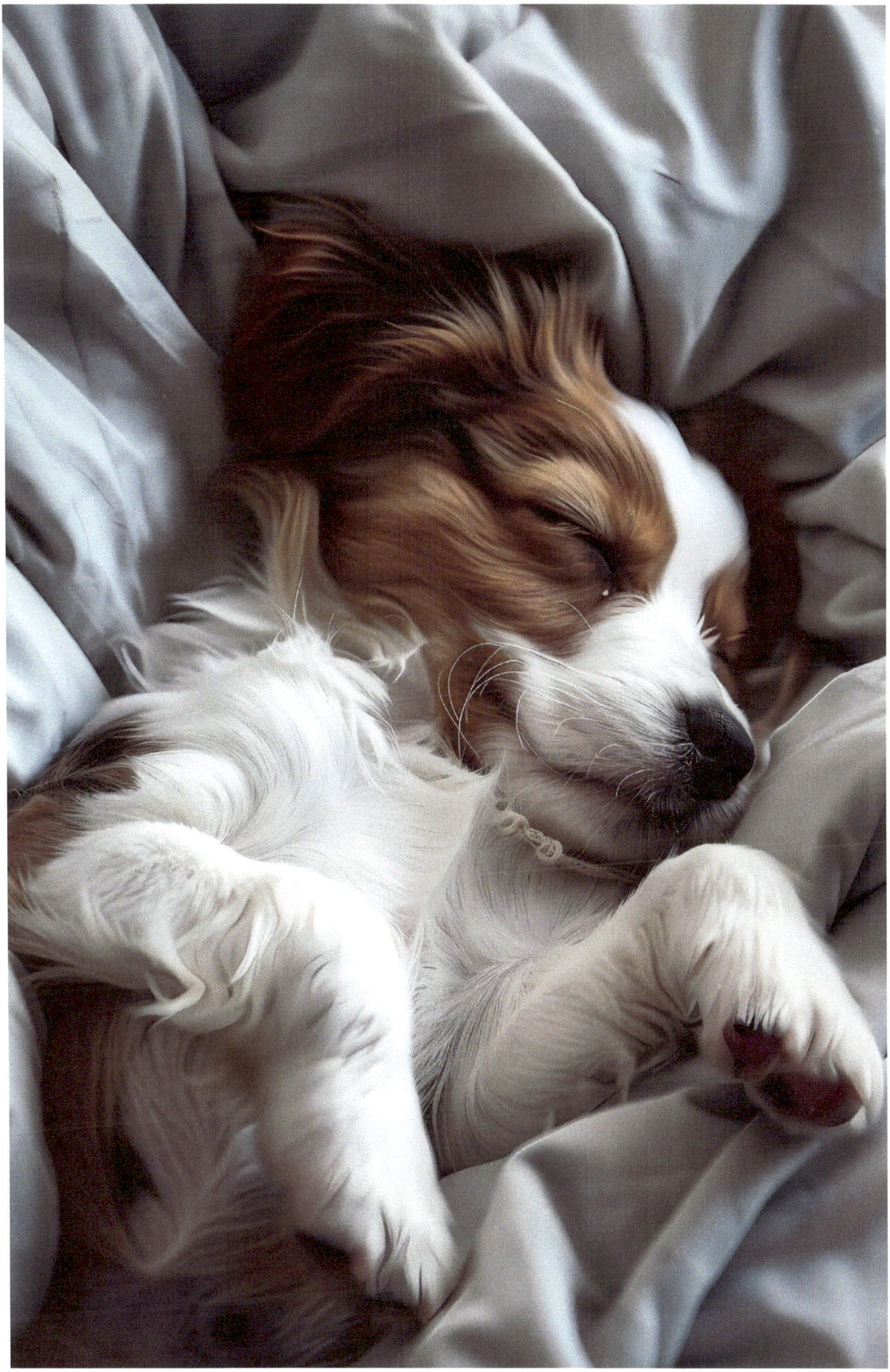

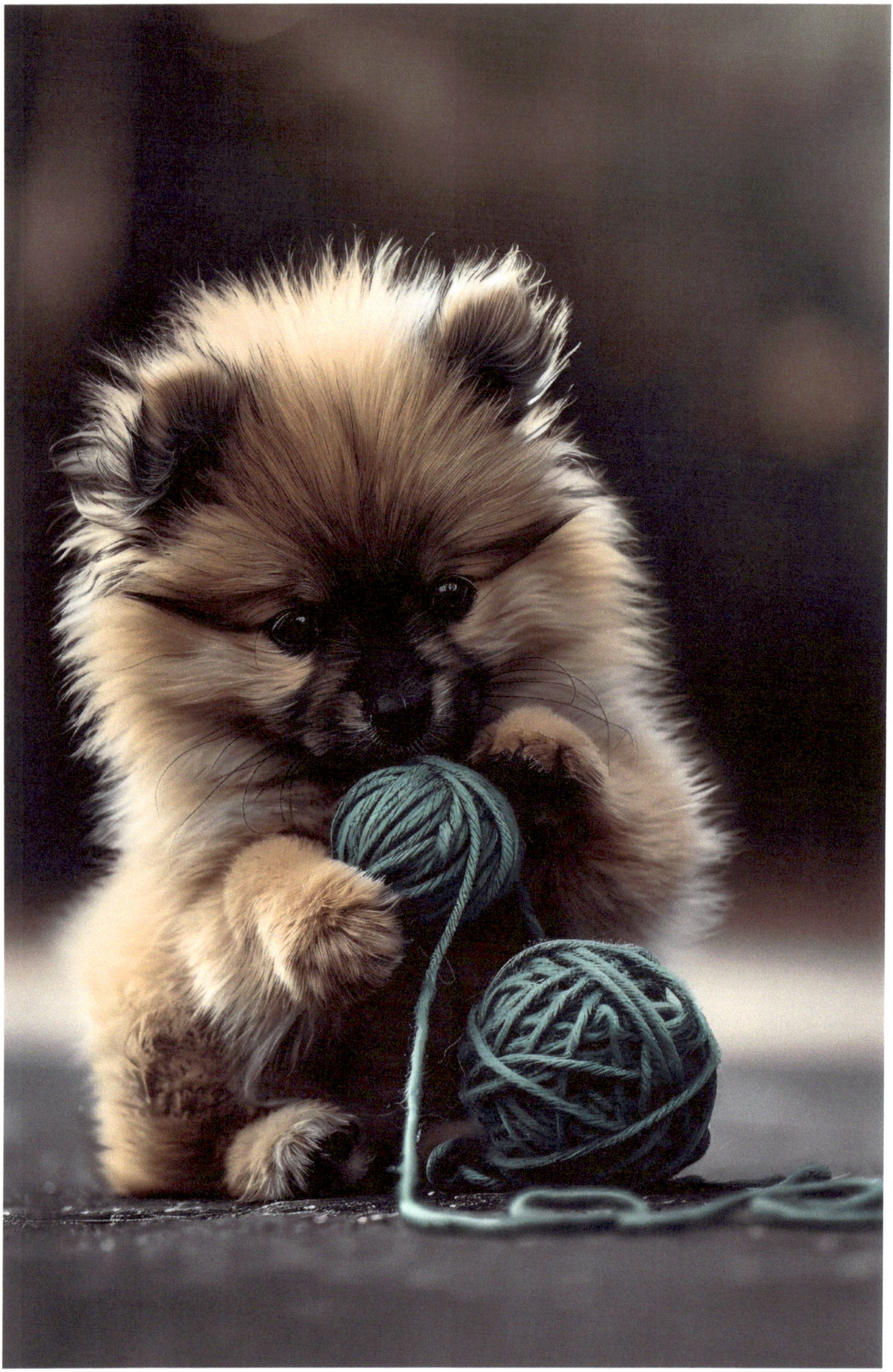

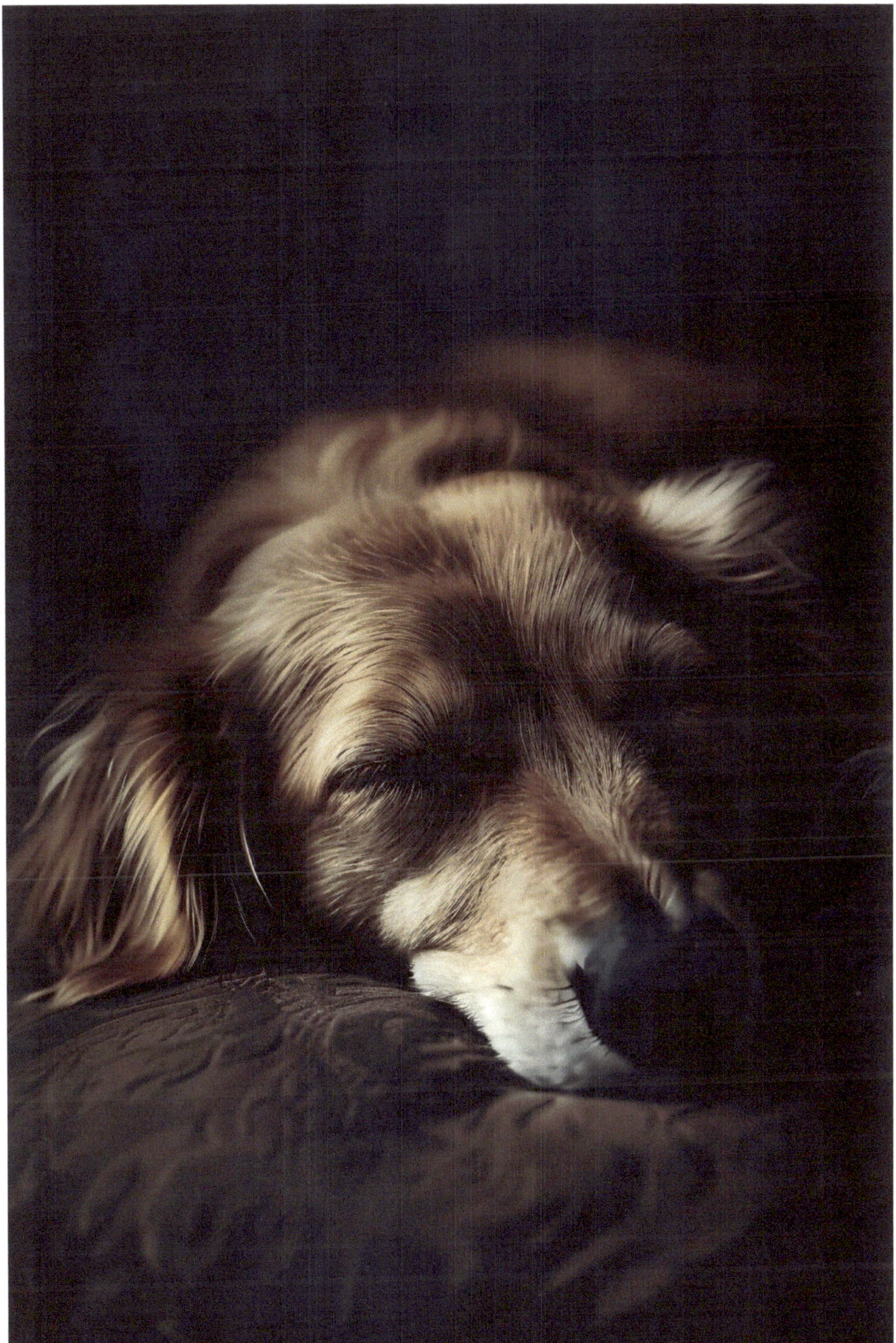

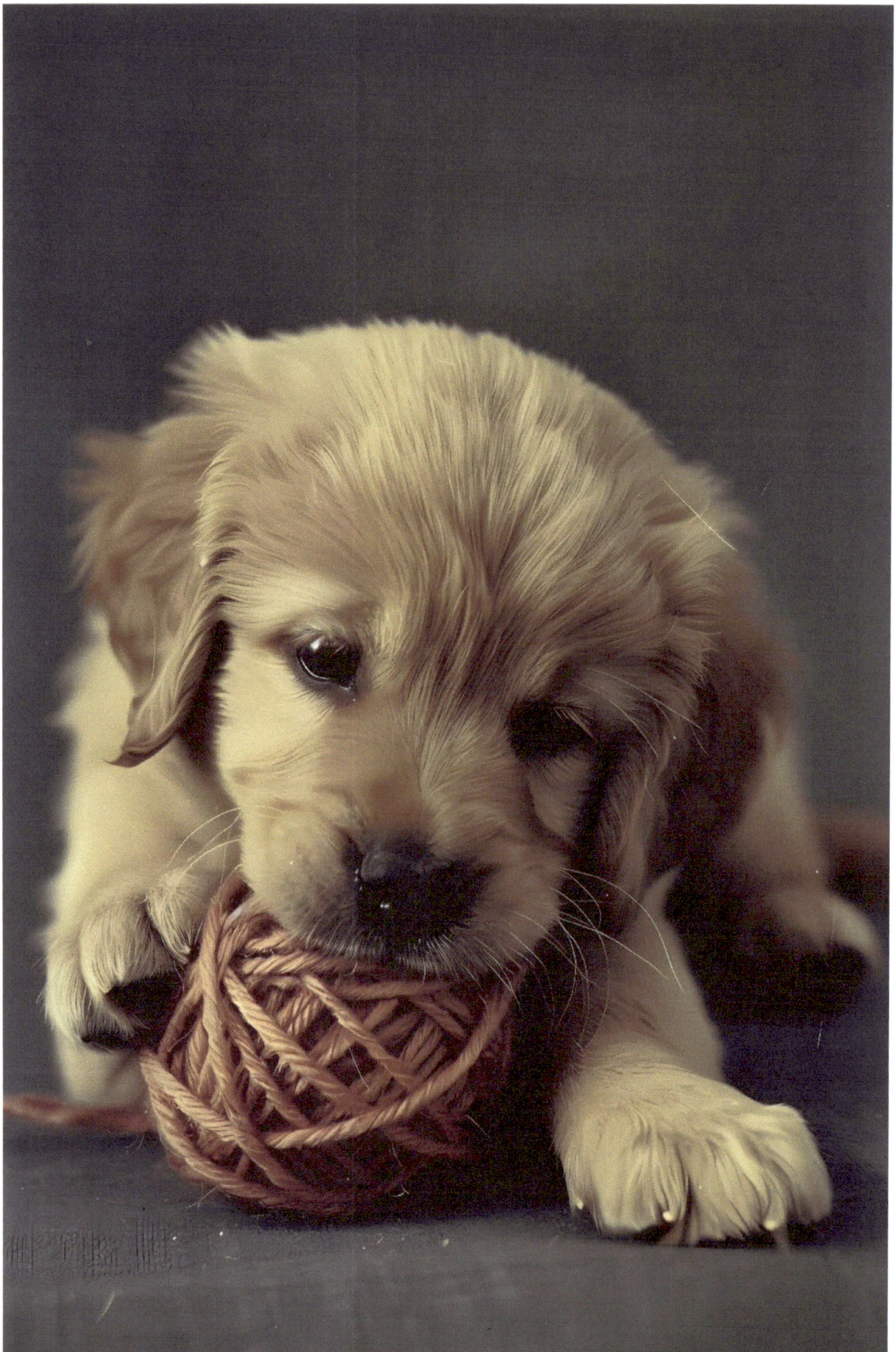

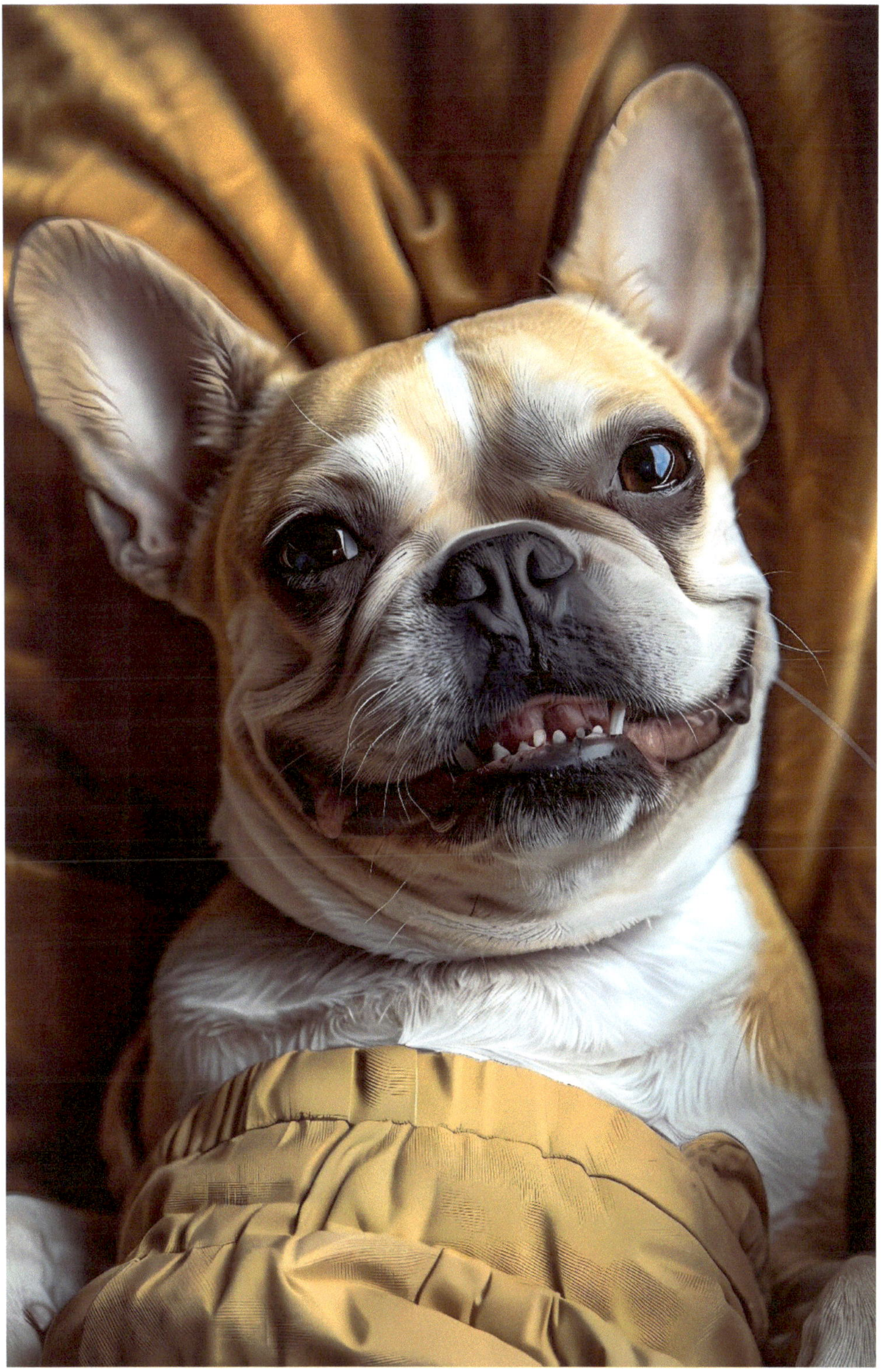

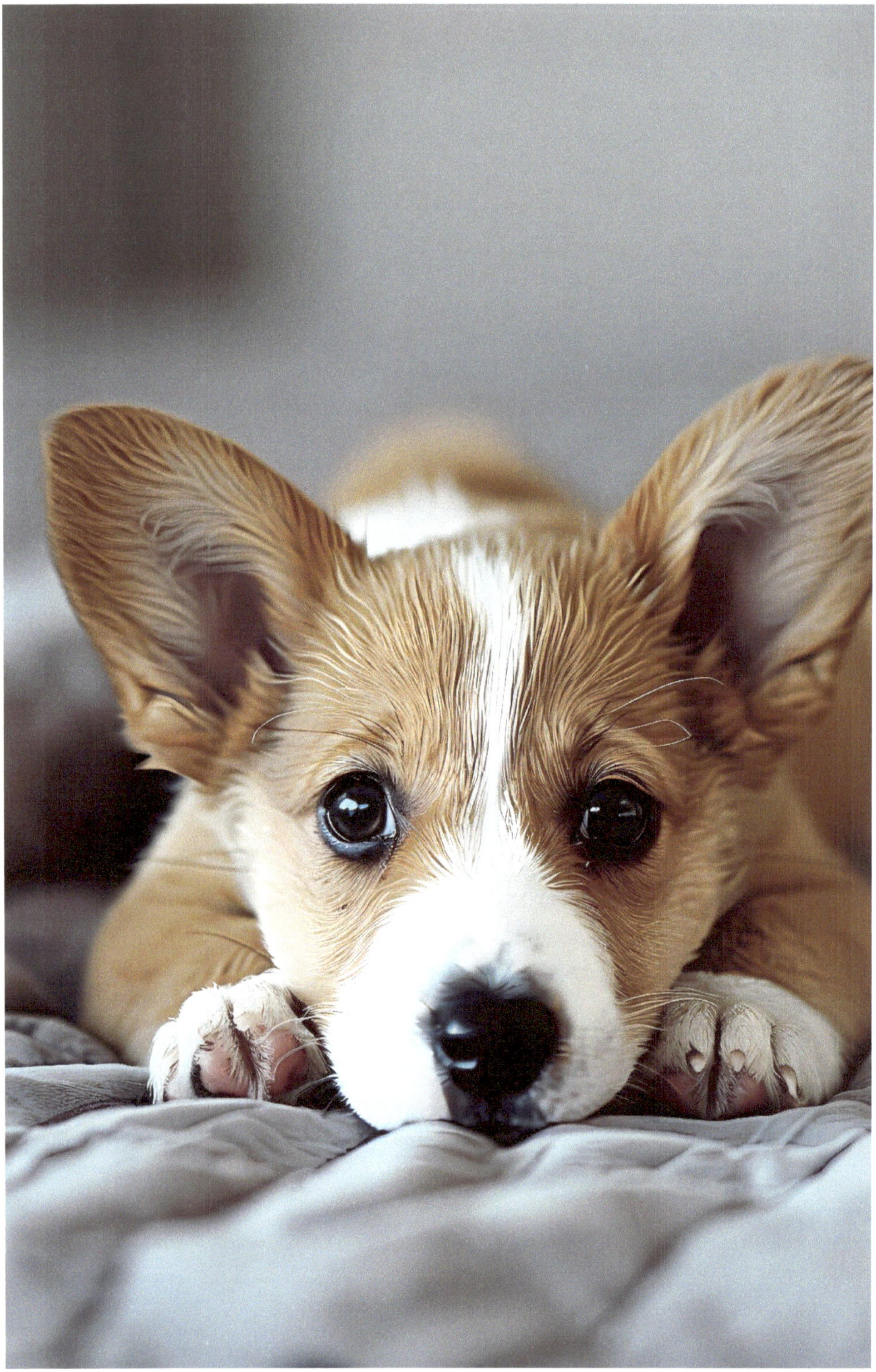

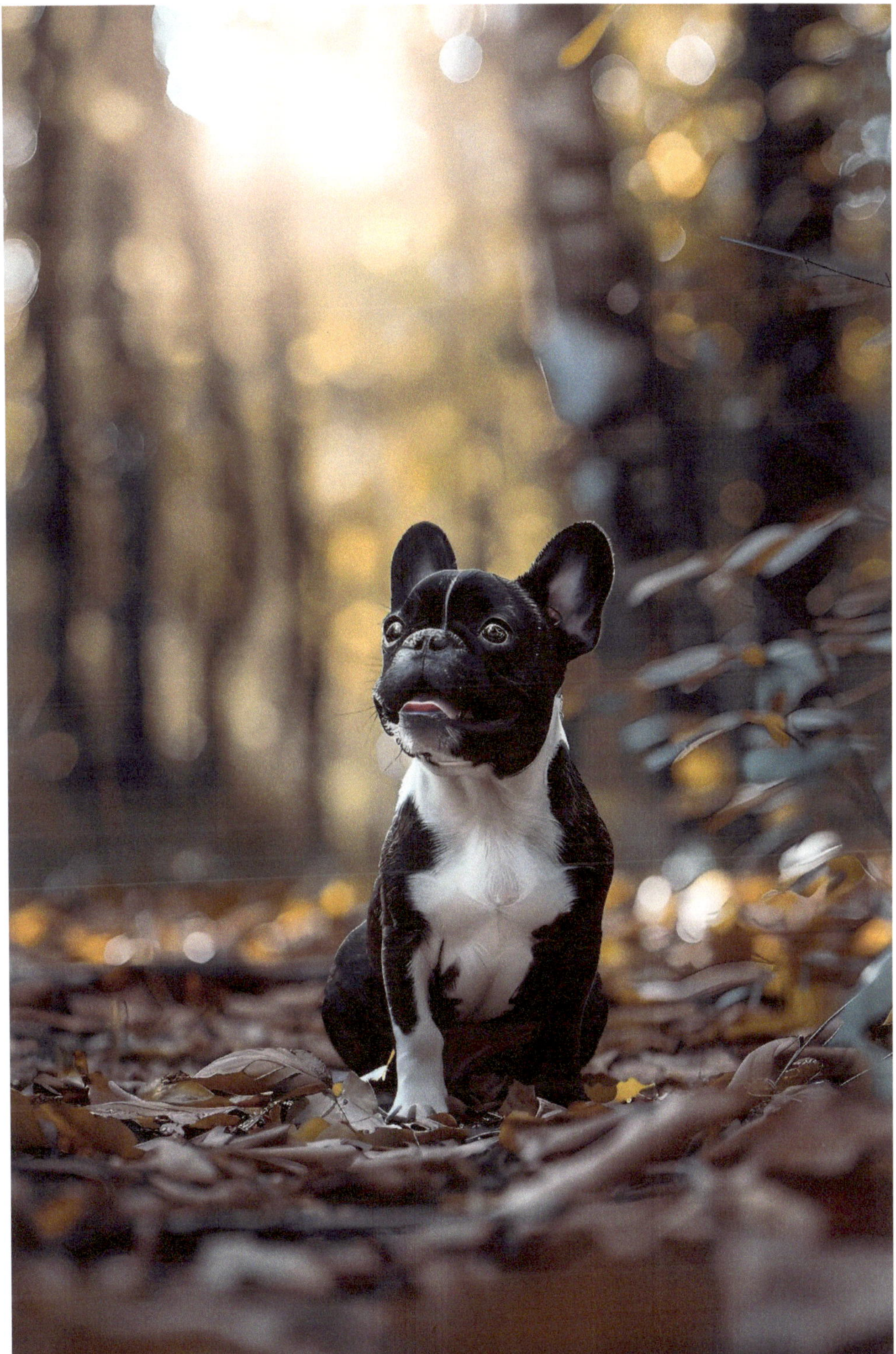

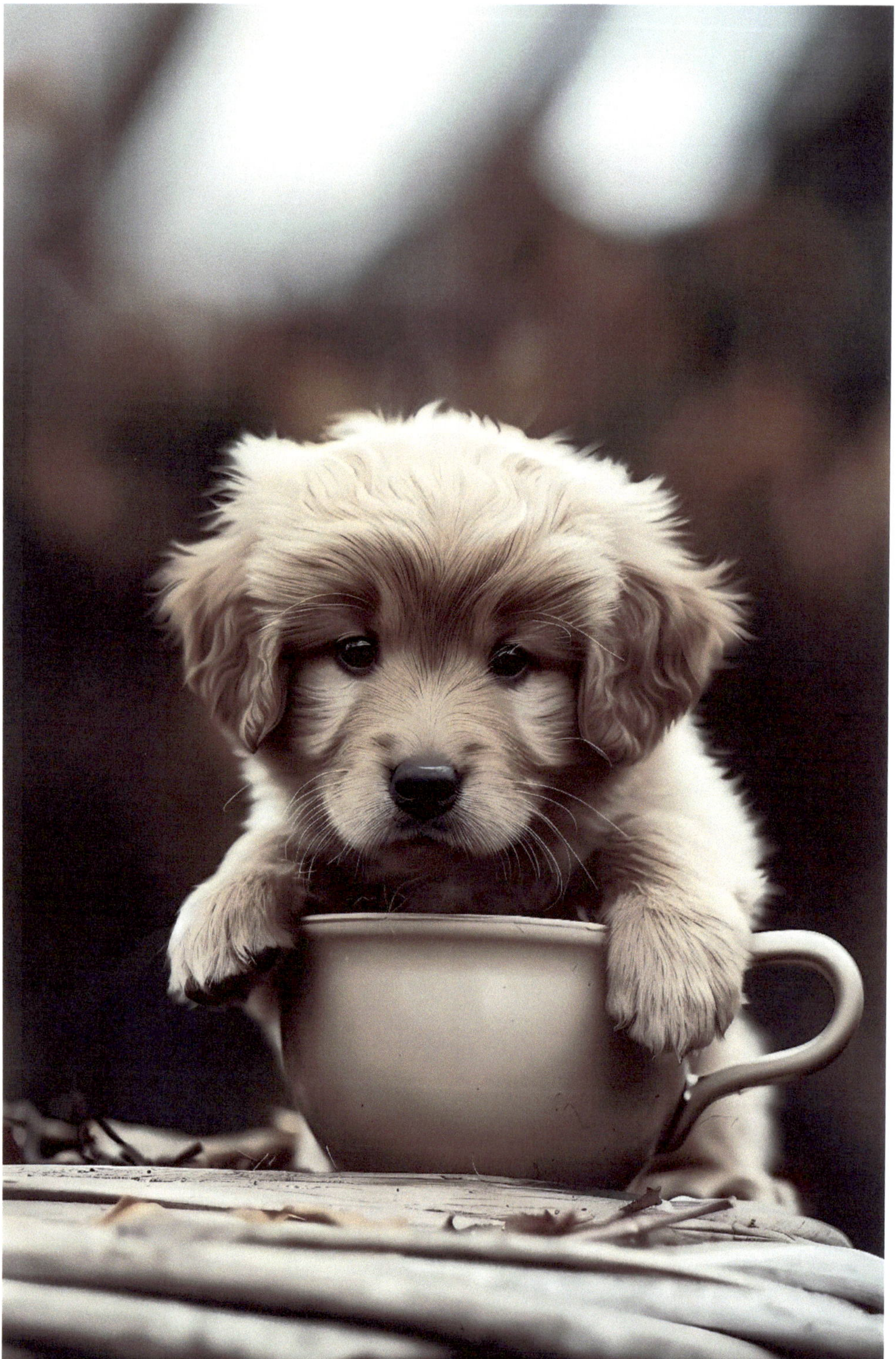

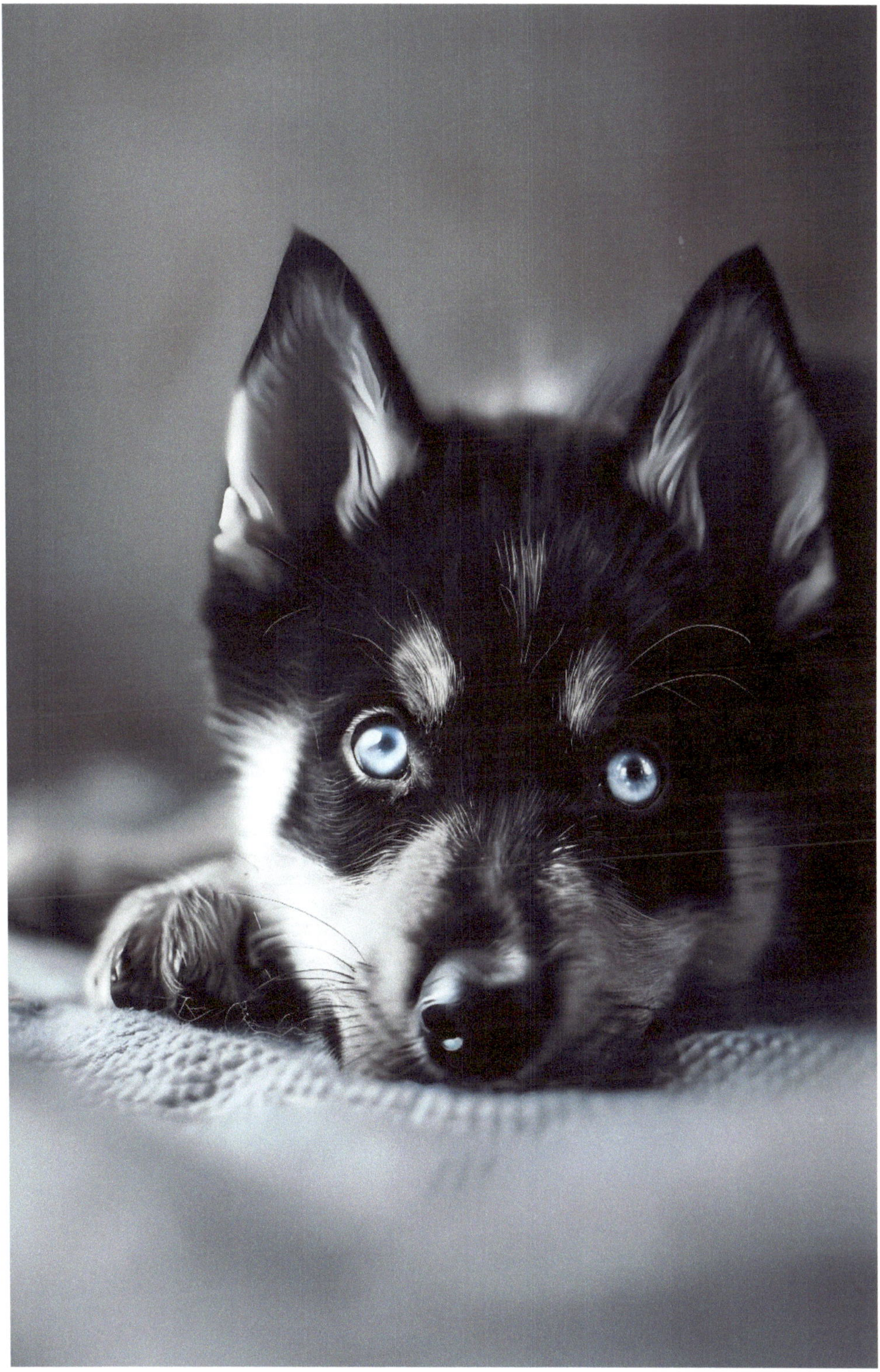

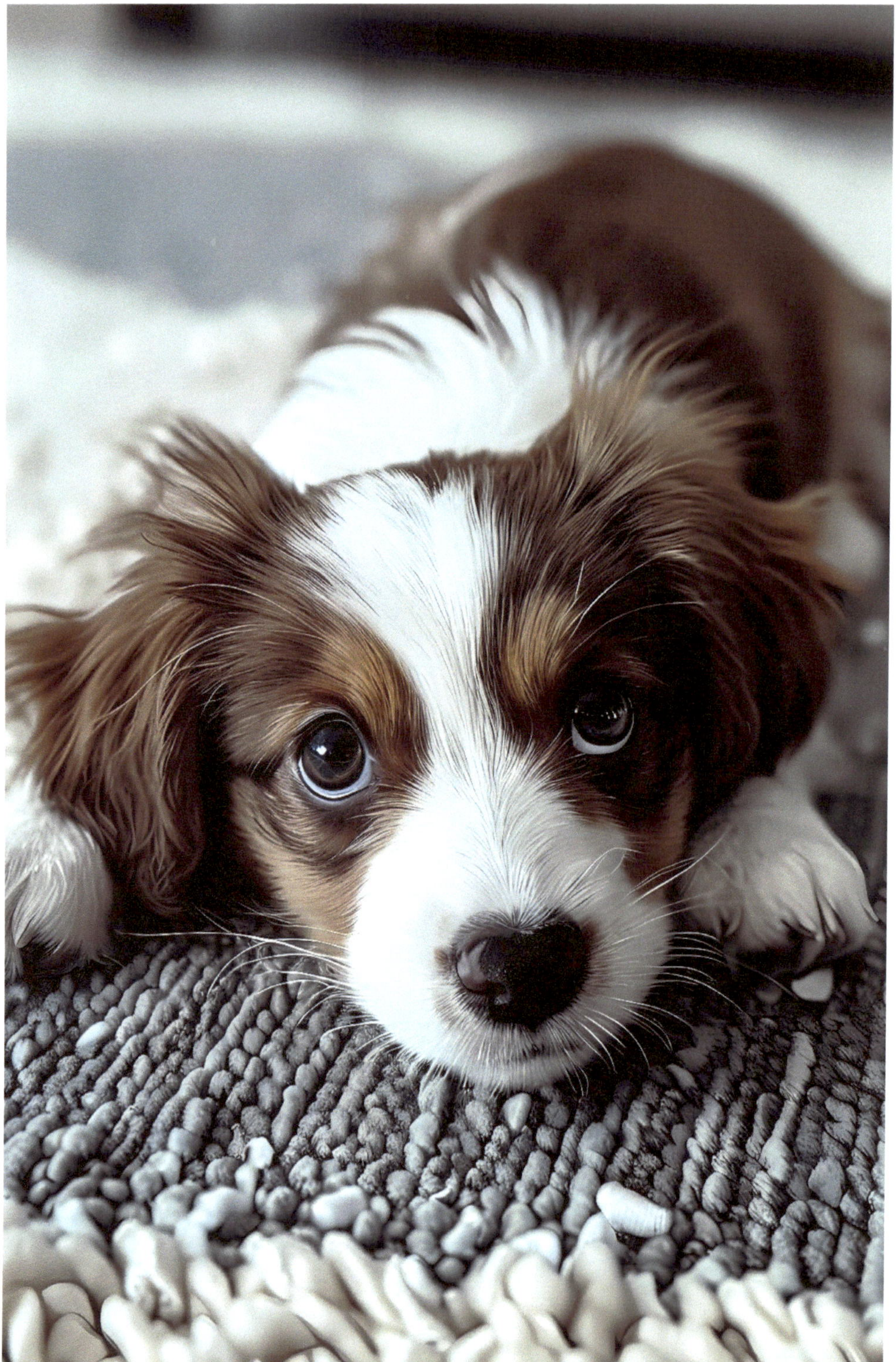

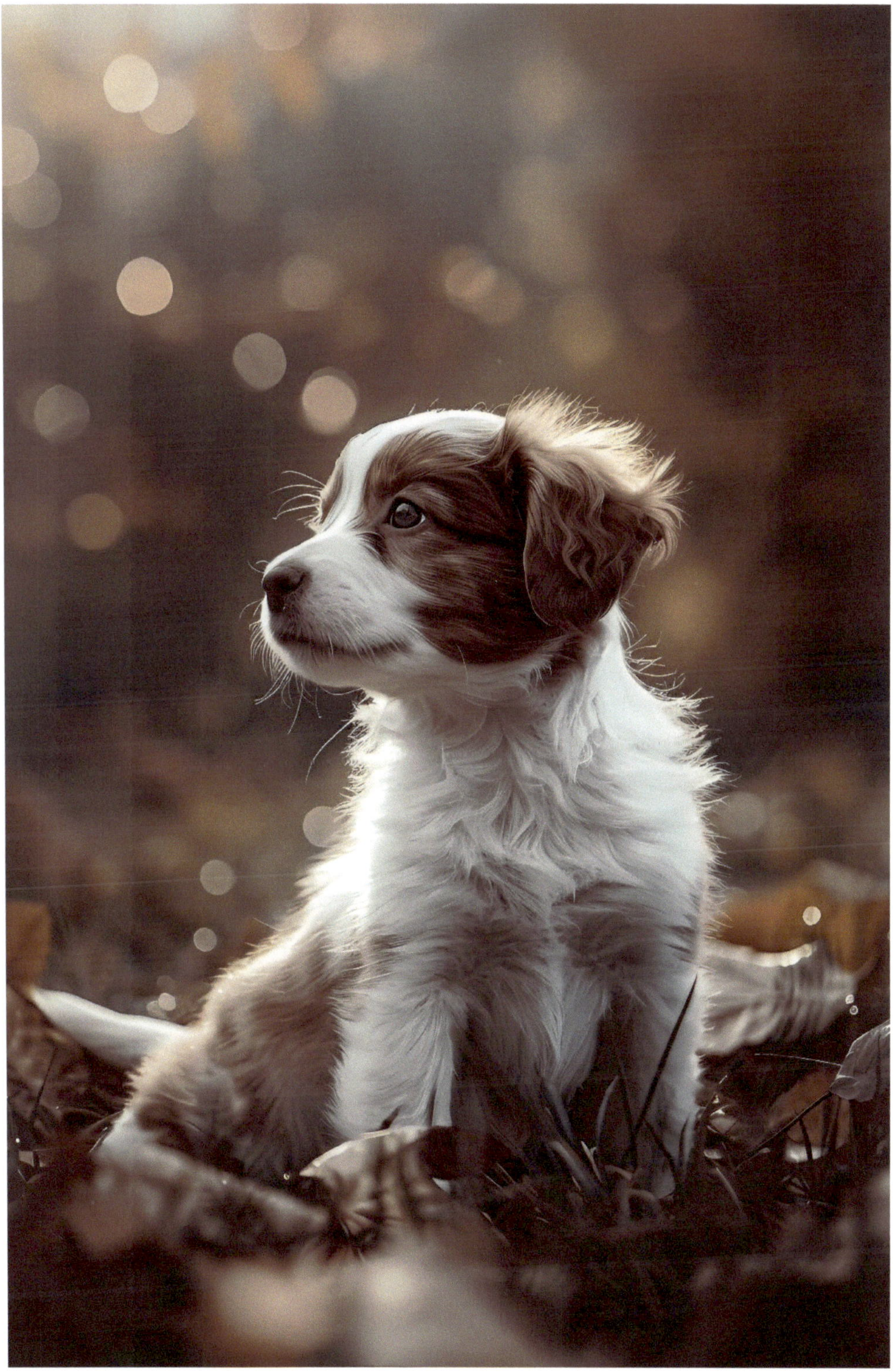

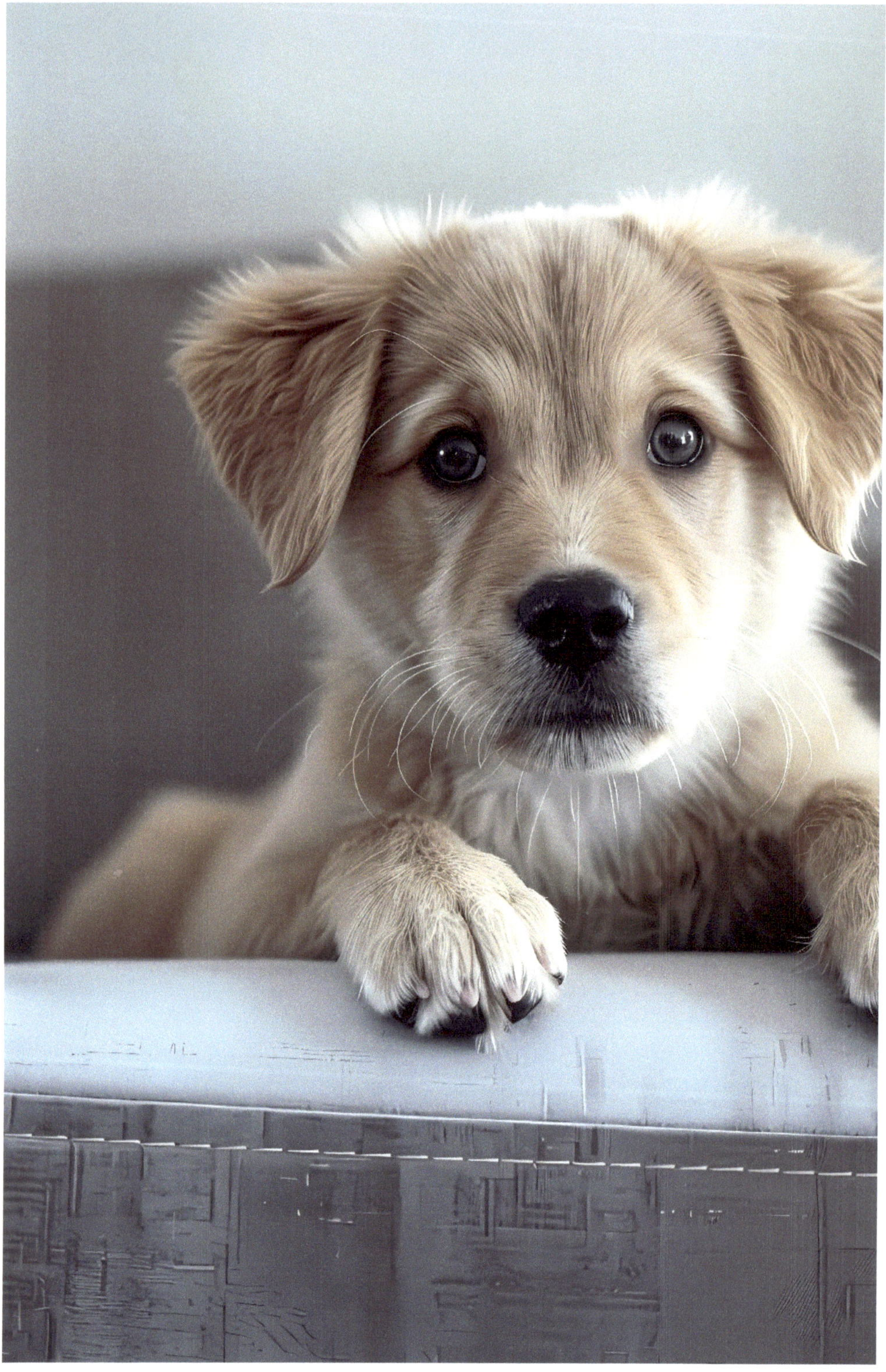

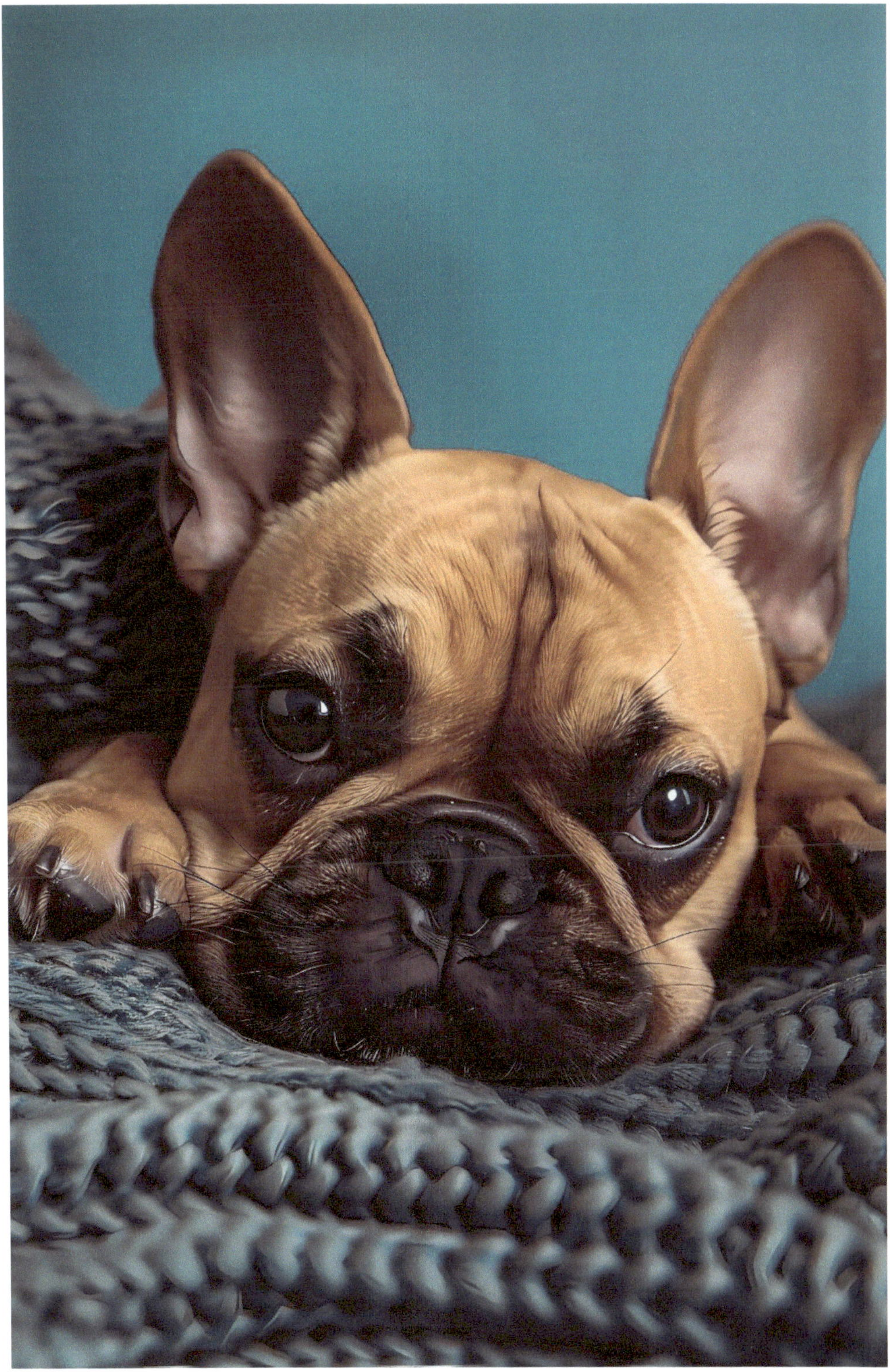

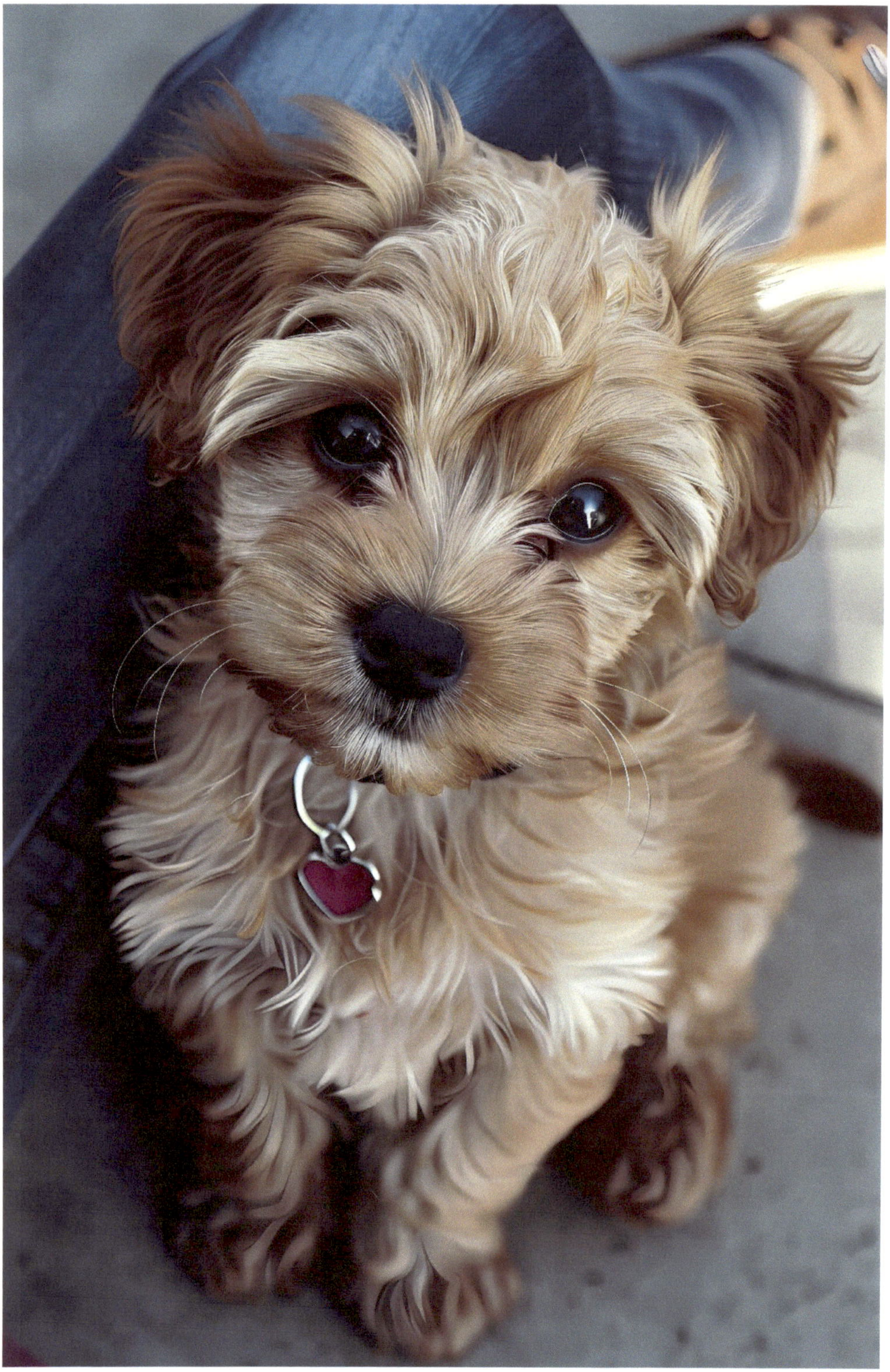

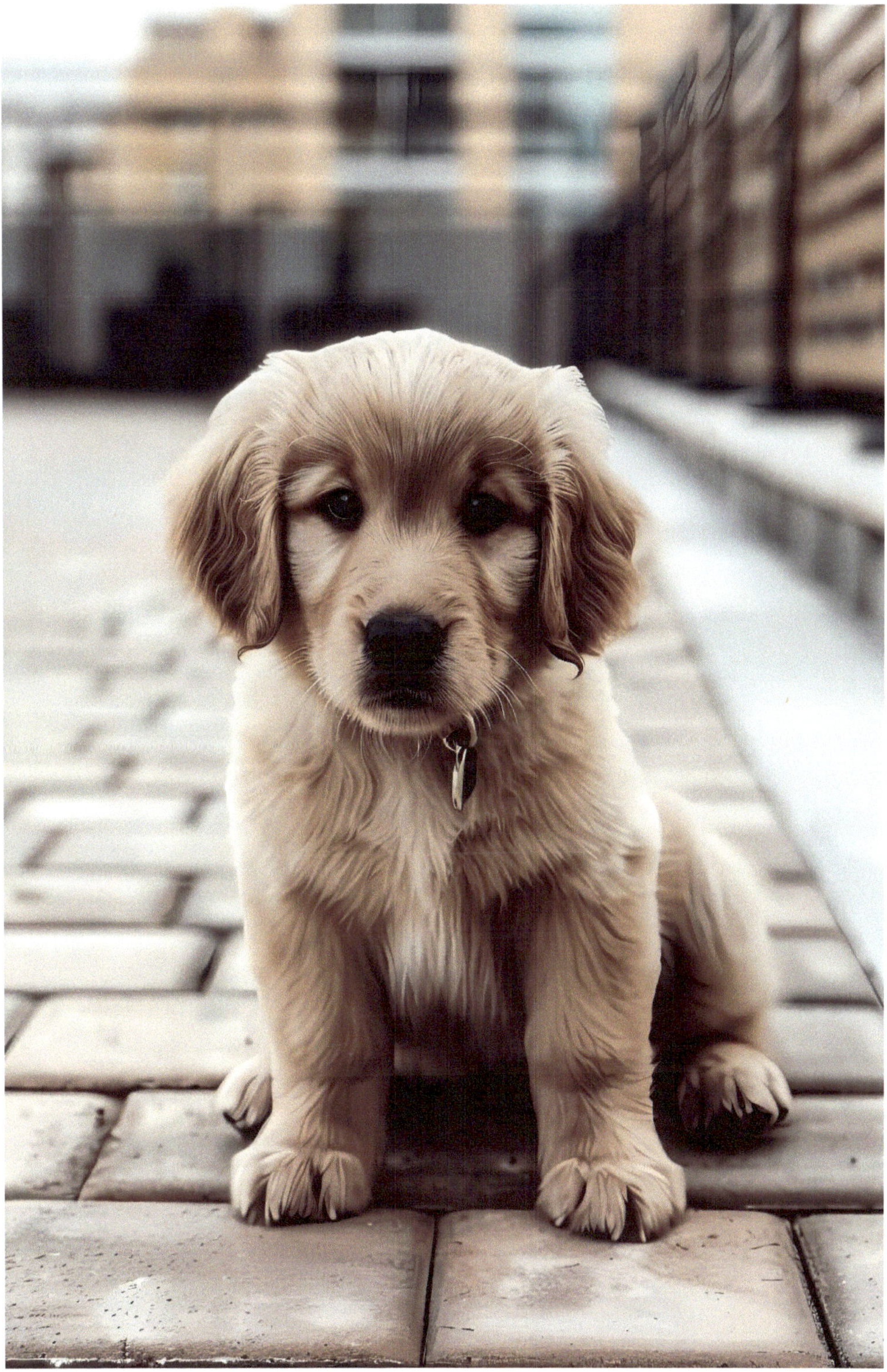

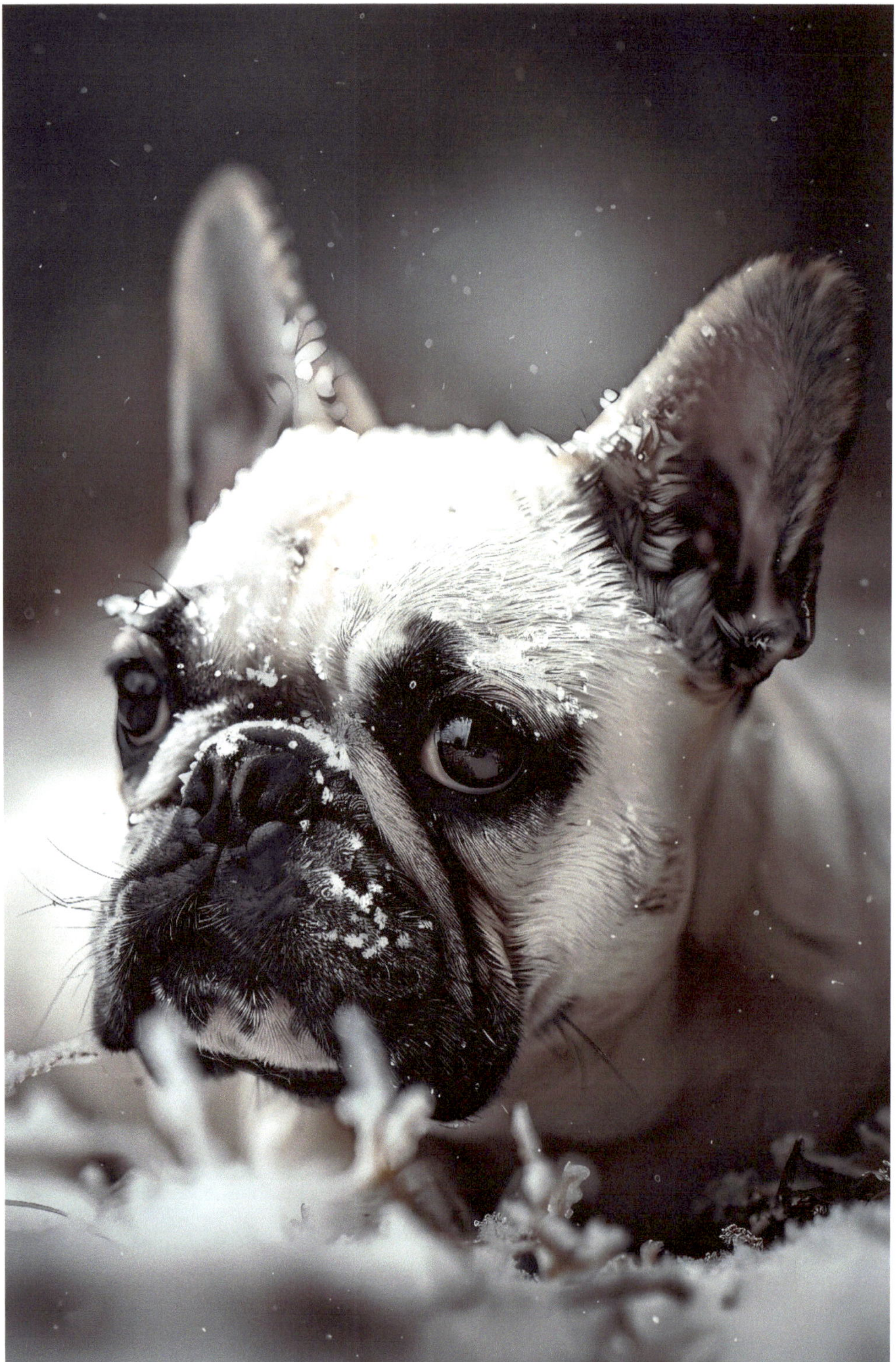

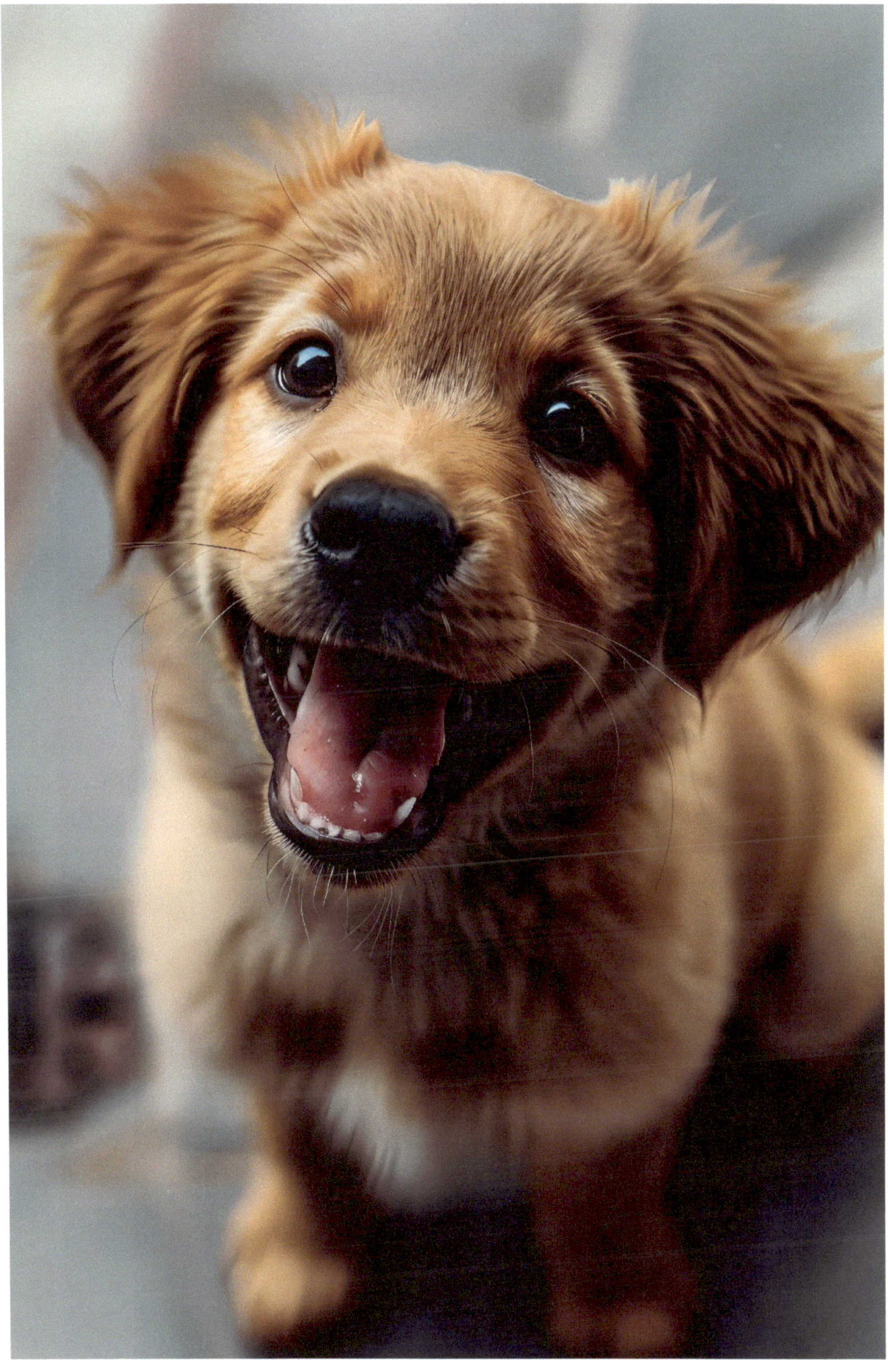

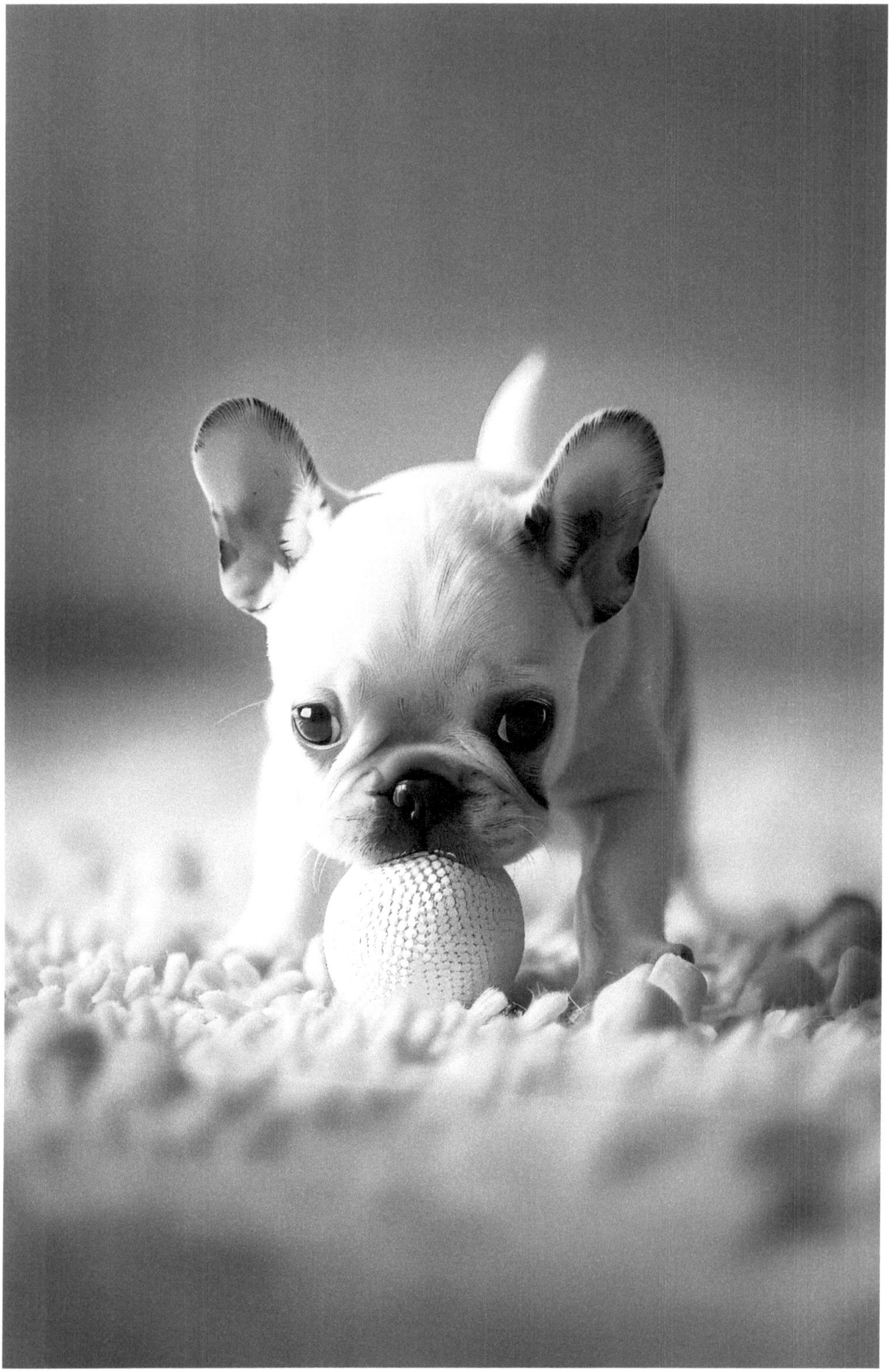

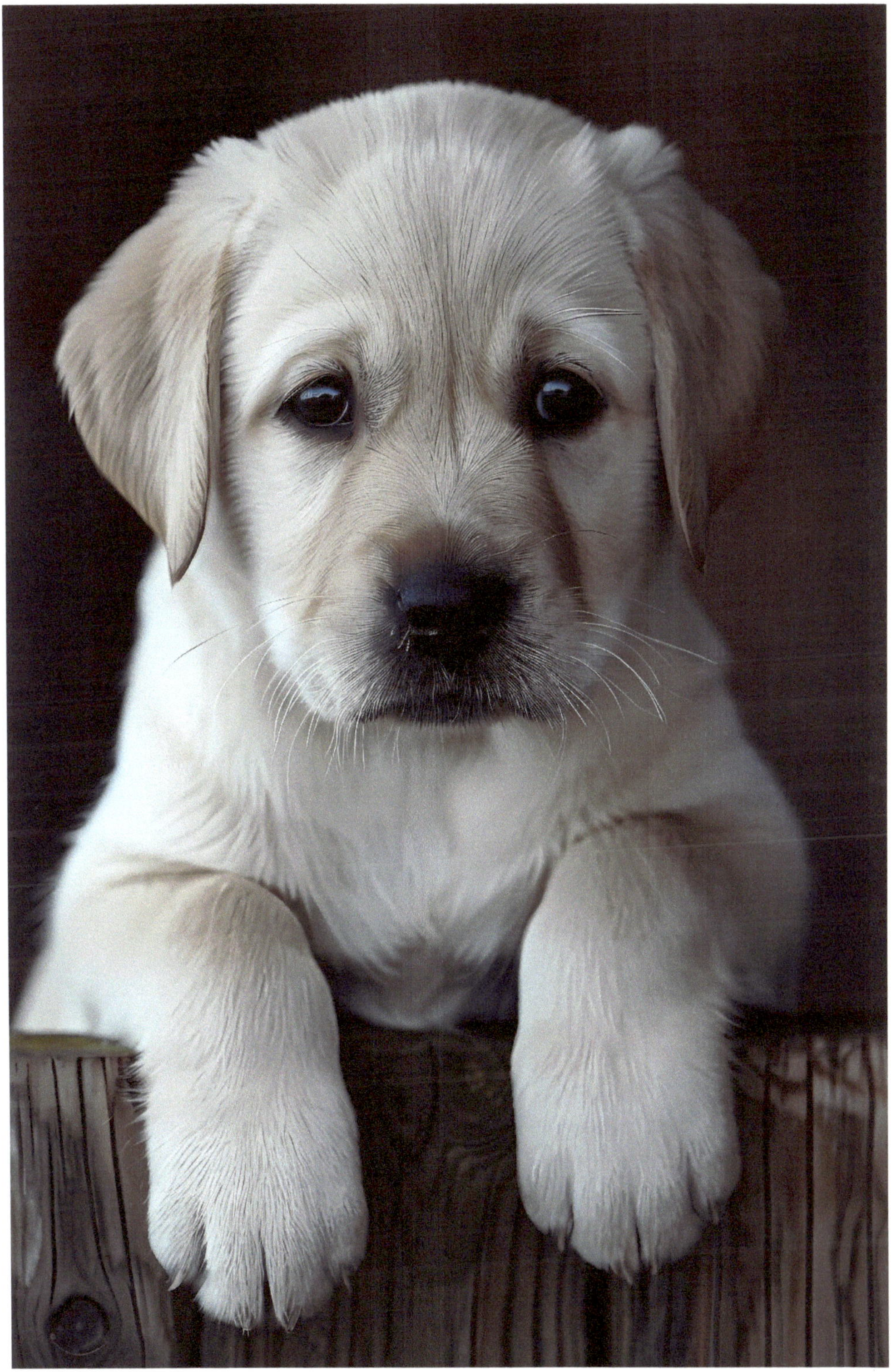

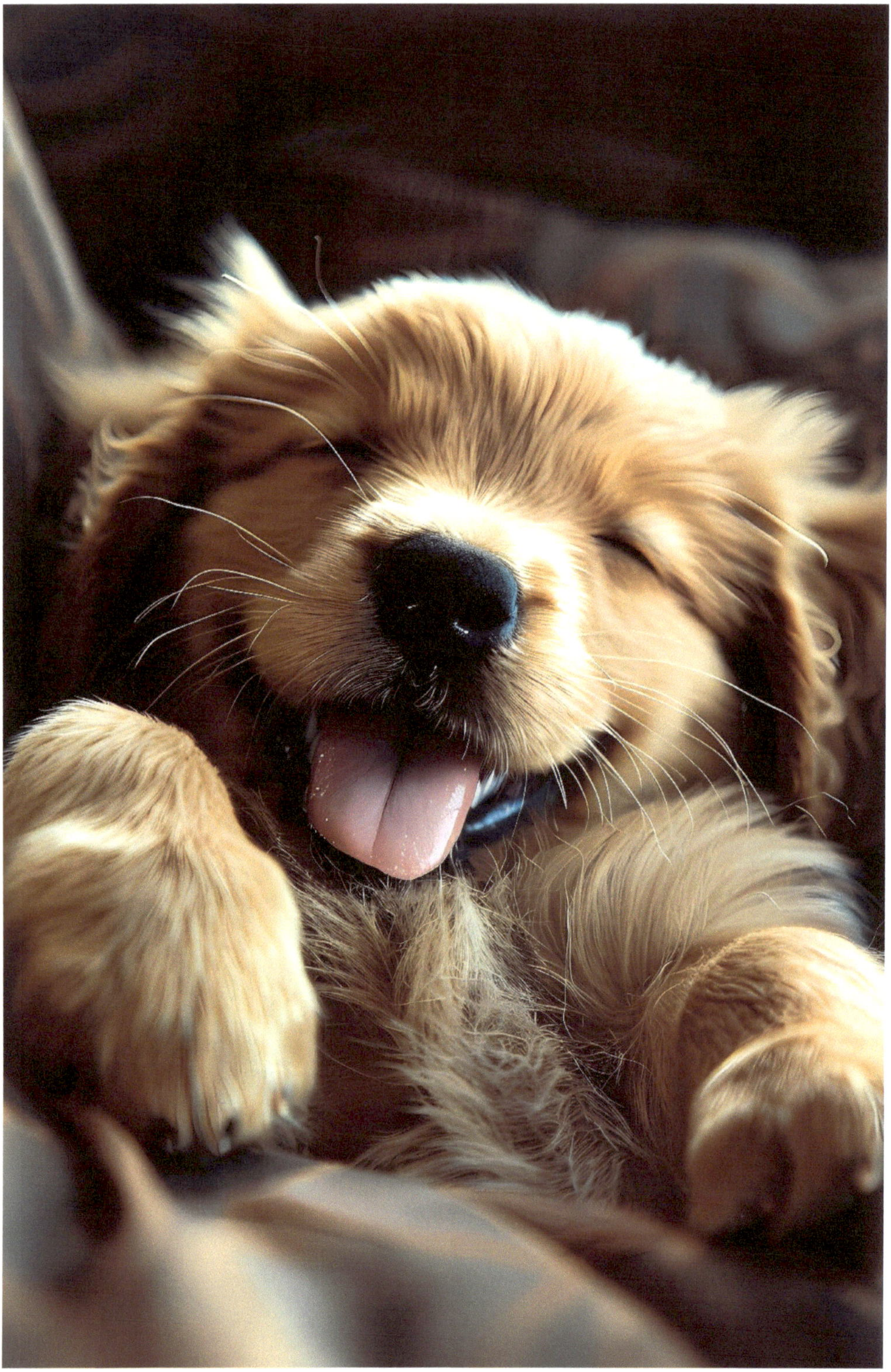

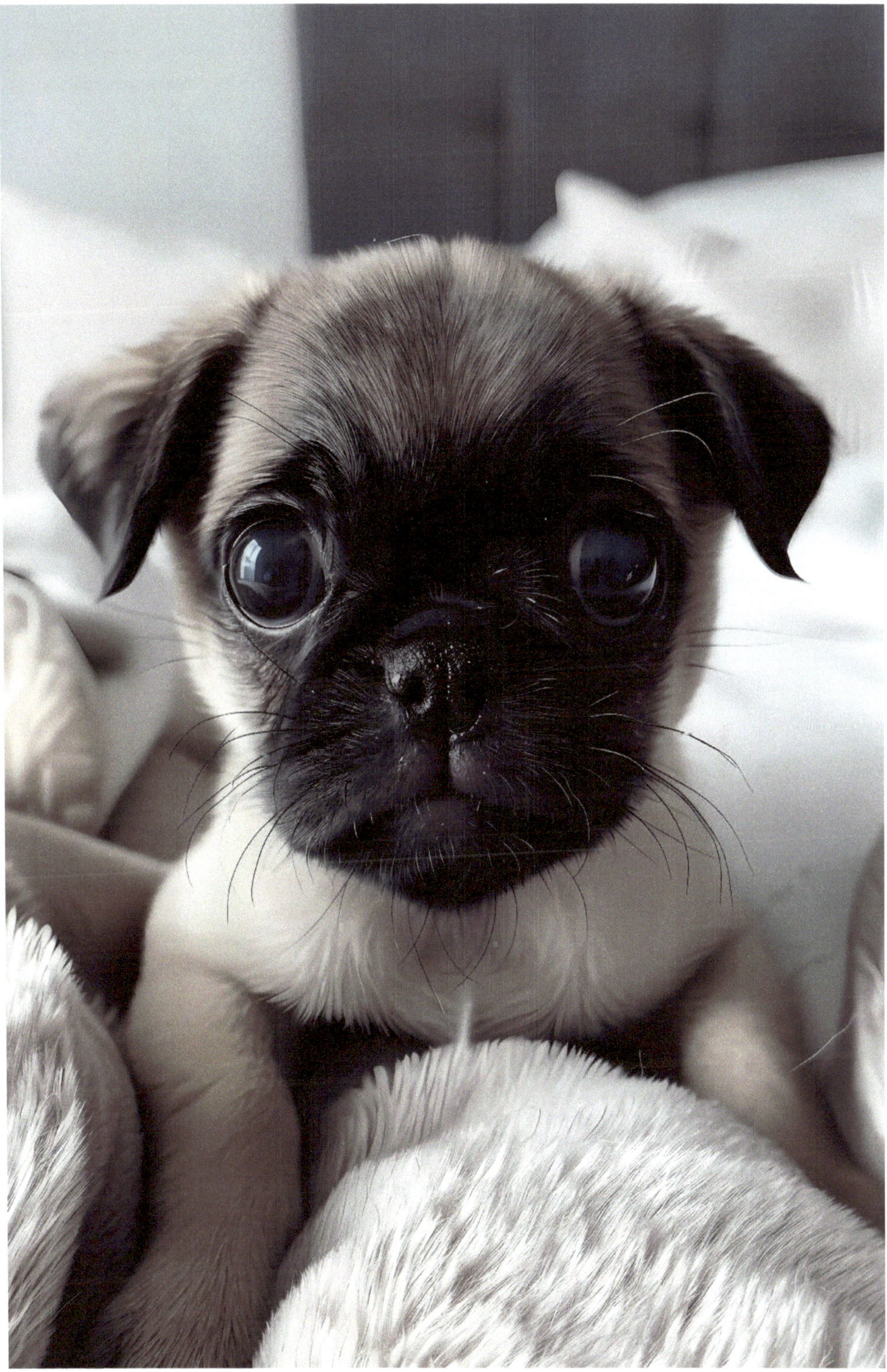

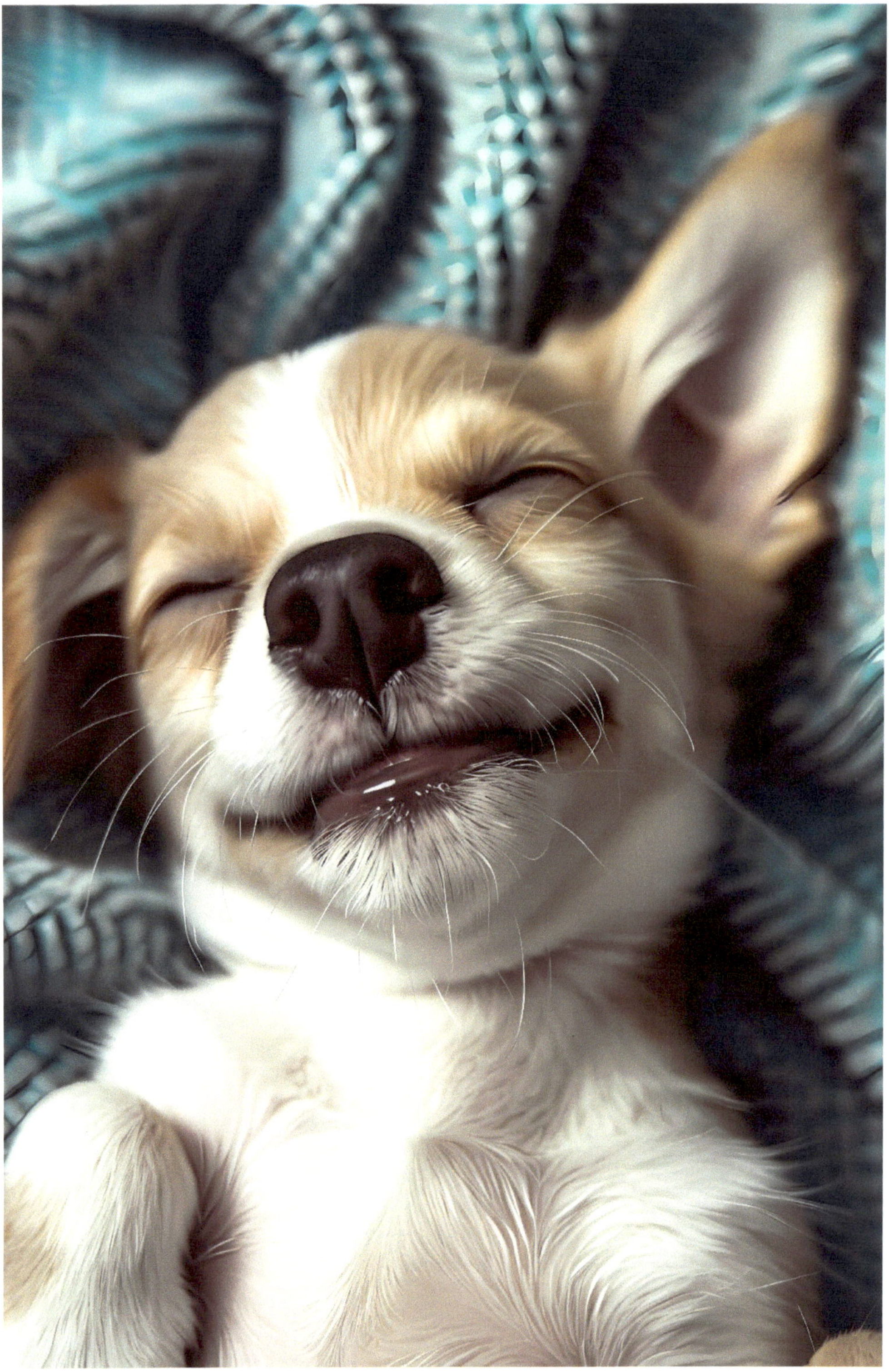

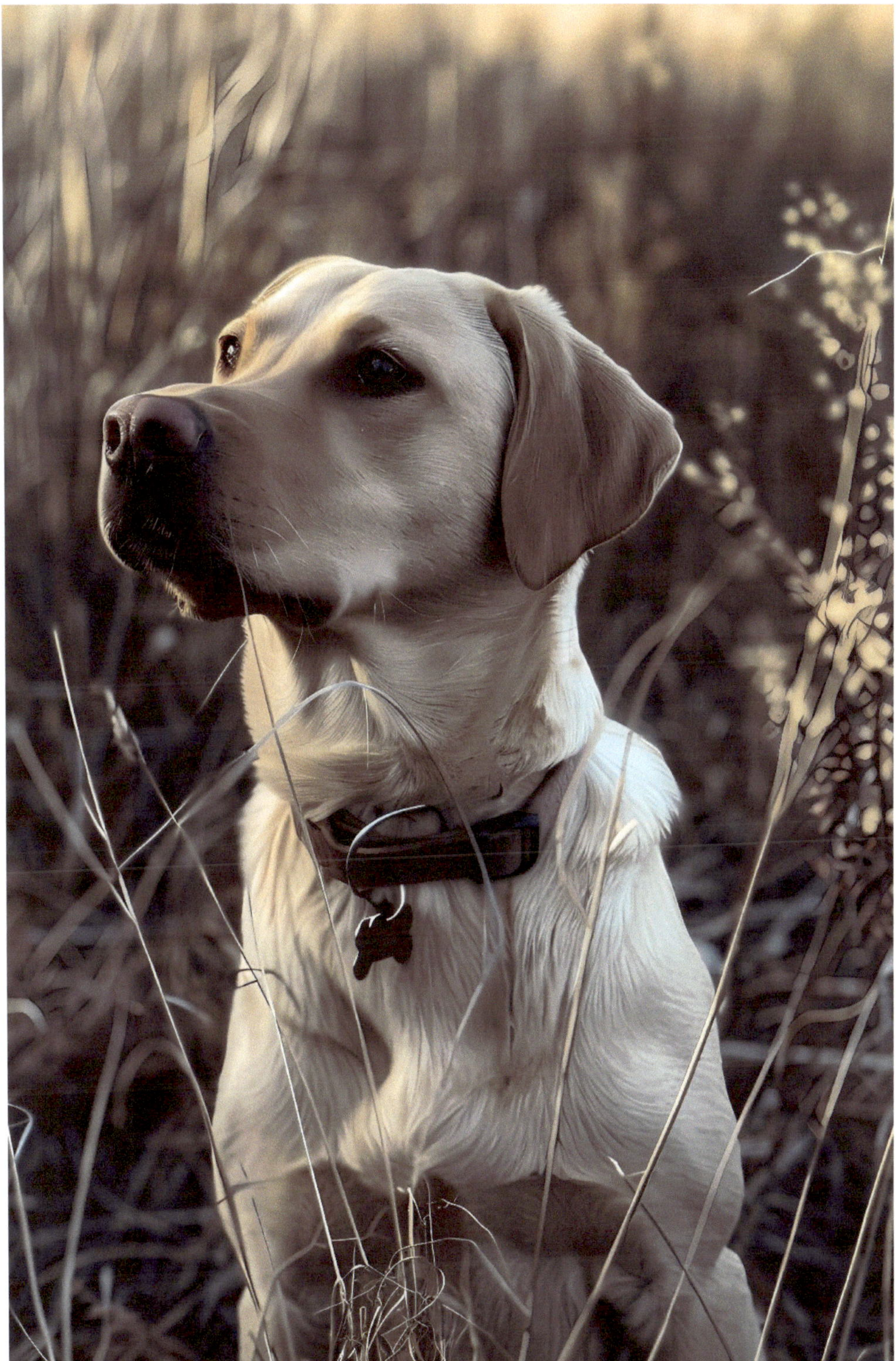

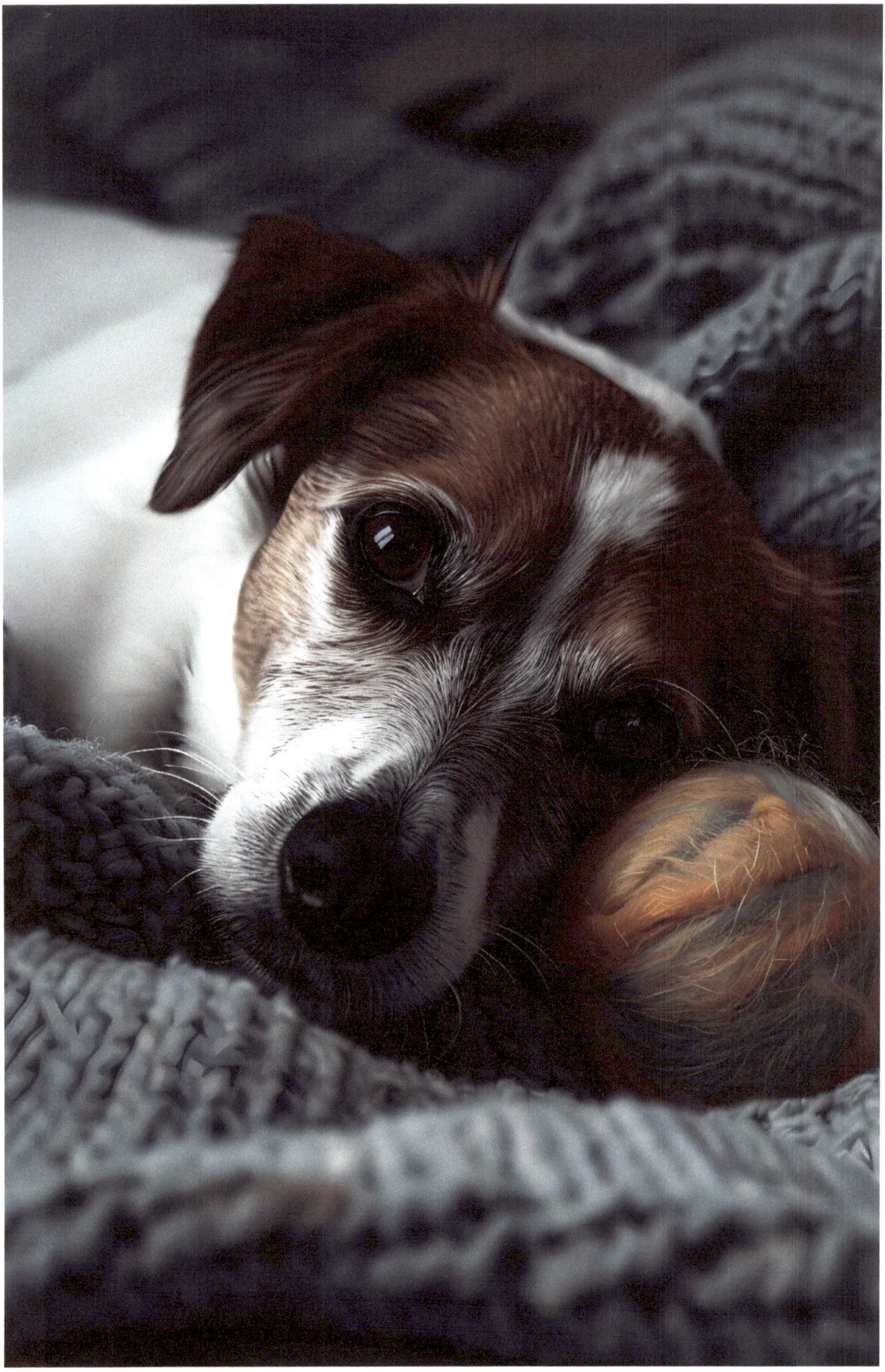

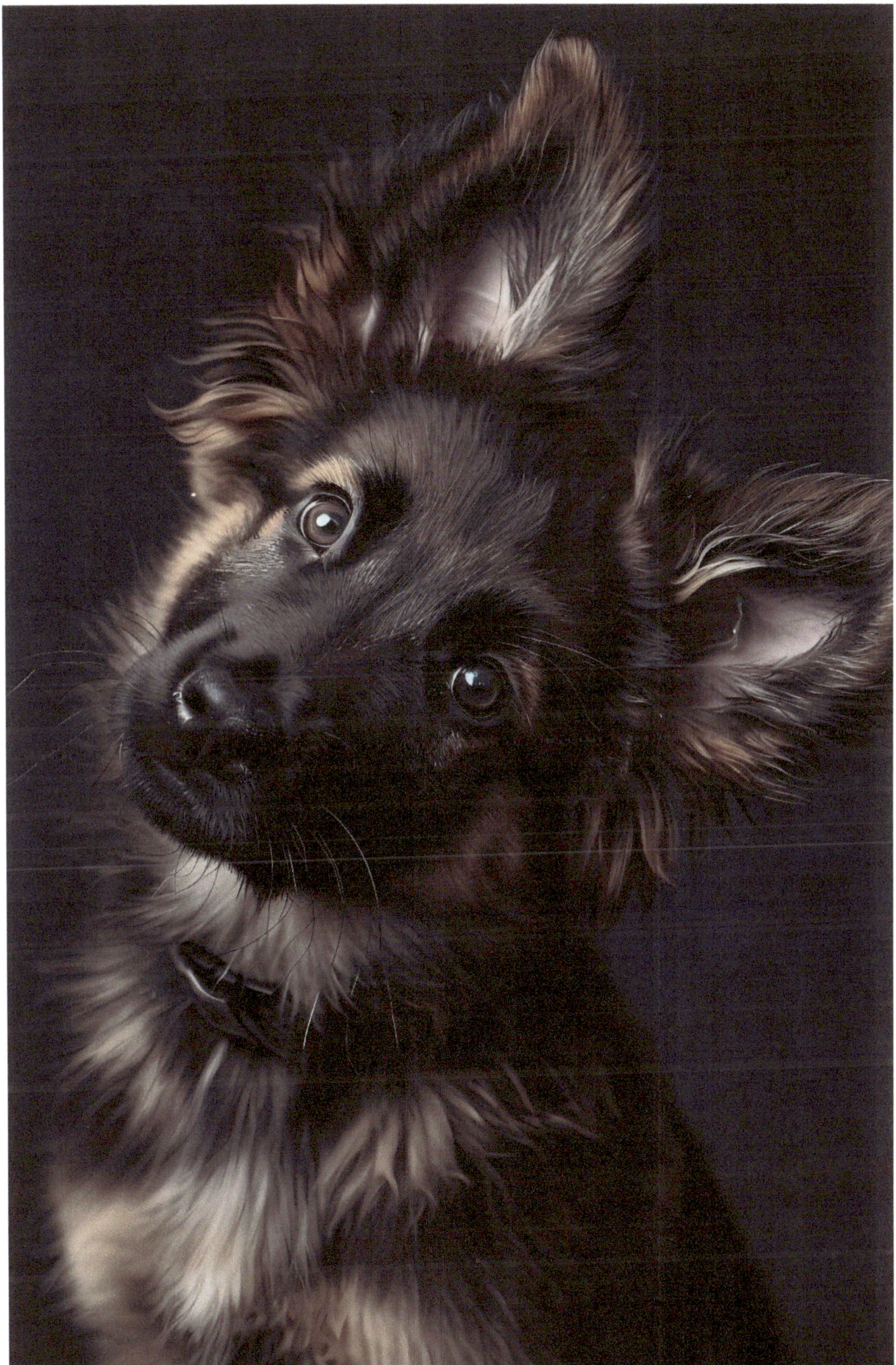

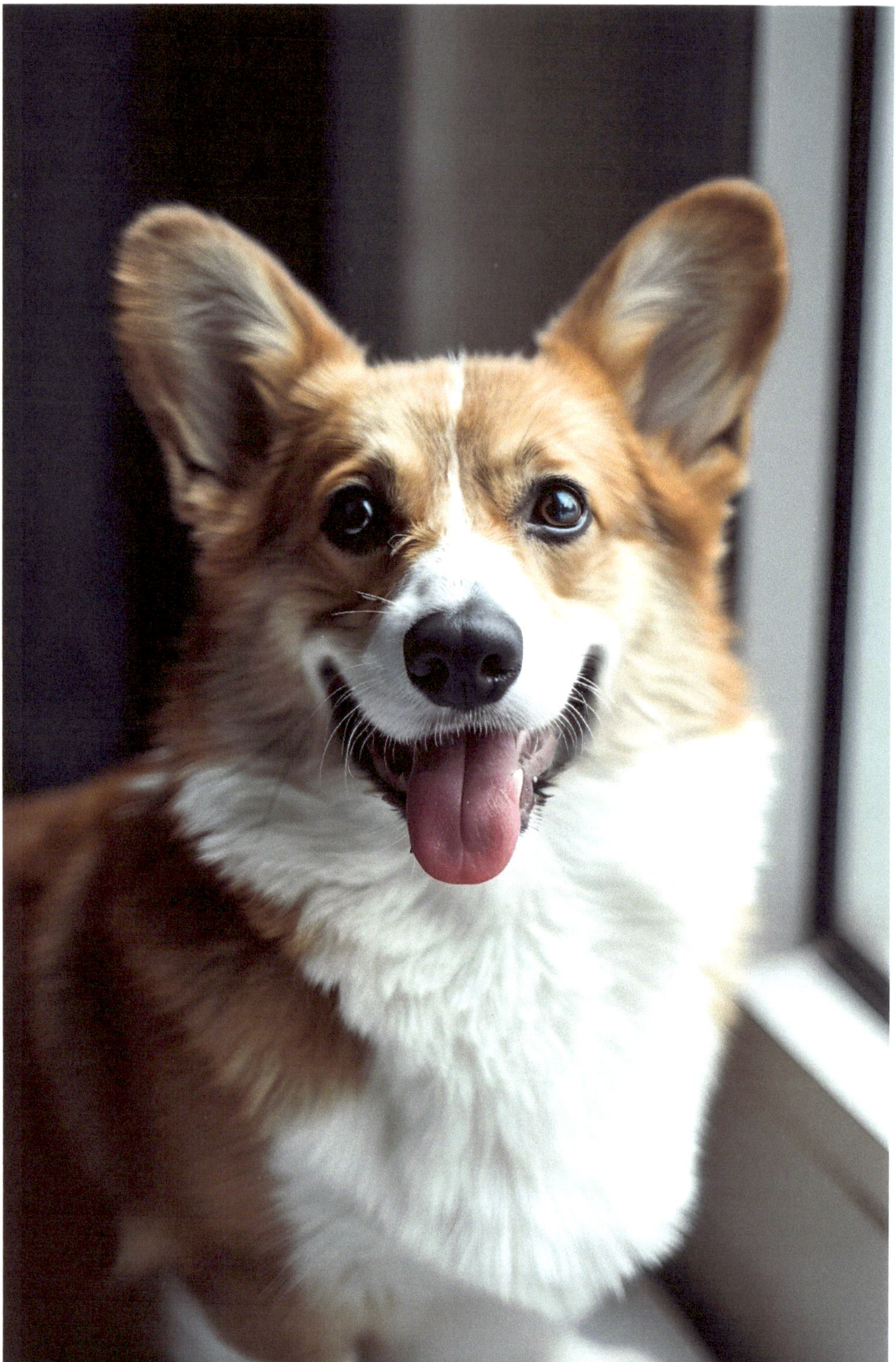

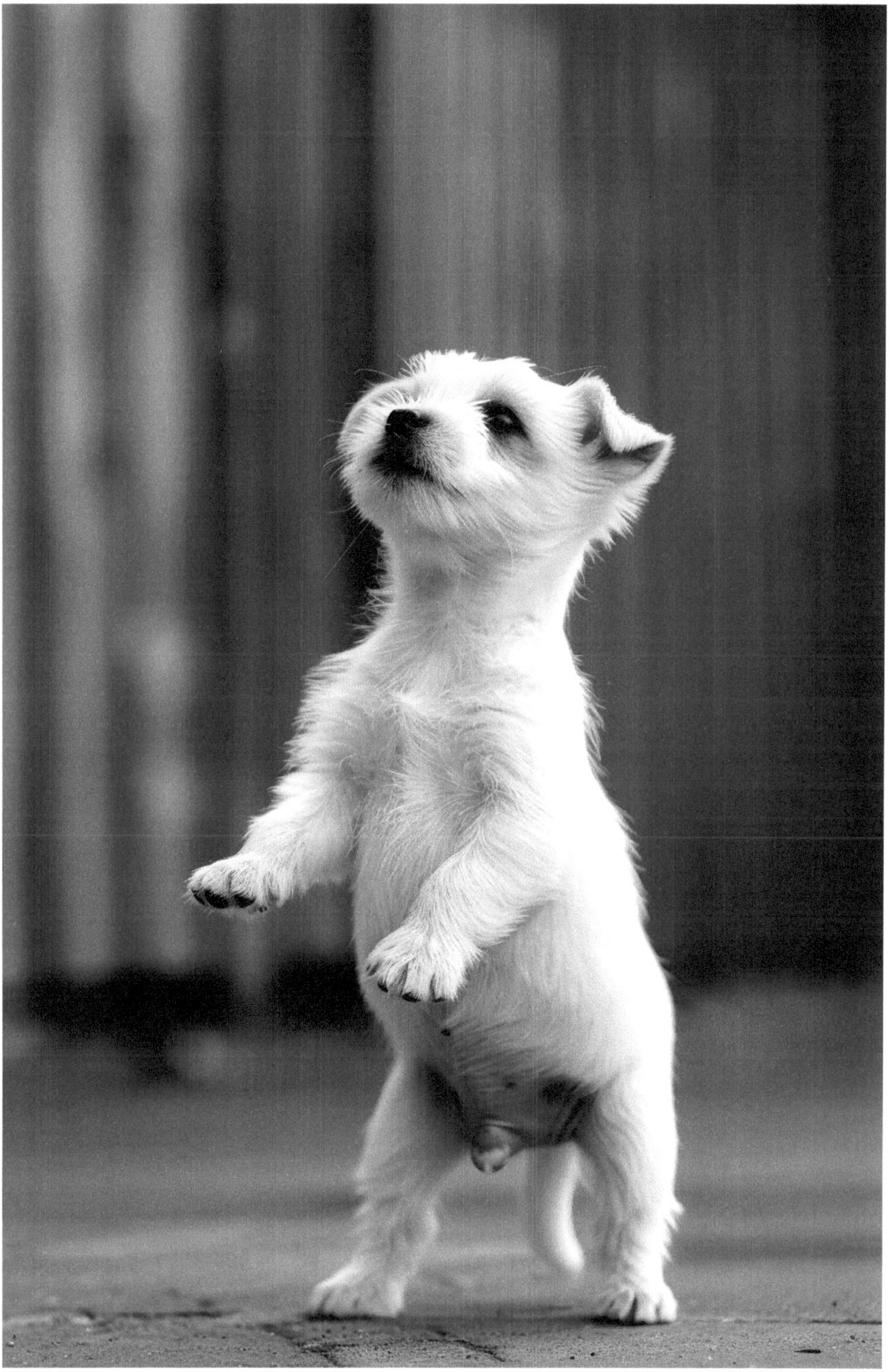

www.ingramcontent.com/pod-product-compliance
Lightning Source LLC
Chambersburg PA
CBHW040335220526
45473CB00009B/2692
9798324057008